T0114031

Praise for *Your Story*

"I love this book! Brimming with candor, wit, and surefire advice, Your Story *by Joanne Fedler is a rich and juicy guide to writing the memoir you've been longing to liberate from your heart. She lays it all out with practicality and leads us within in service of putting it out there. If you are compelled to bring Your Story to the page, and you're looking for tips, courage, and answers, look no further, everything you're seeking is right here."*

—— Nancy Levin, author of *Worthy*

"Your story can change someone's life. Fedler's message is a powerful reminder that ordinary stories of growth, healing, and transformation are the medicine this world needs now, and that each human life has its place in the great unfolding narrative of our planet. A book that inspires hope and teaches each of us how to use our words to leave a legacy."

— Van Jones, CNN contributor and *New York Times* best-selling author of *Green Collar Economy* and *Rebuild the Dream*

"My favorite line from any book ever is the very last line from Charlotte's Web . . . 'It is not often that someone comes along who is a true friend and a good writer. Charlotte was both.' . . . which is what came to me as I dove in to the first chapters of Your Story. *Joanne Fedler is a true friend to her reader, and an amazing writer. She is also a brilliant teacher. Get this book if you've ever dreamed of writing a book. It will not only elevate your spirit and teach you that your experiences, your heart, and your soul are a rich and worthy voice—but it will show you exactly how to capture that voice in the written word."*

— Christine Kane, president and founder of Uplevel You

"*Joanne Fedler is a compassionate word tour guide on the bumpy journey into writing. Her book is a comforting companion for writers as they navigate the joys and sorrows of their internal landscape. Joanne understands the writer's loneliness and desperate need for belonging. In this book, she has created a menu of encouraging possibilities on how to overcome our fears and dig deep into our souls, so that our true voice can emerge. Thank you, Joanne, for reminding us that though we are writing from our story, we are writing for others.*"

— Nava Semel, award-winning author and playwright

"*[This book] has been life changing, perhaps one of the best books I've ever read on writing. Now to actually do some writing!*"

— Kevin Ritchie, regional Executive Editor, Gauteng & Northern Cape, *The Star*, South Africa

Your Story

ALSO BY JOANNE FEDLER

The Dreamcloth
It Doesn't Have to Be So Hard
The Knot List
Love in the Time of Contempt

The Reunion
The Secret Mothers' Club
Things without a Name
When Hungry, Eat

Your Story

HOW TO WRITE IT
SO OTHERS WILL
WANT TO READ IT

Joanne Fedler

HAY HOUSE, INC.
Carlsbad, California • New York City
London • Sydney • New Delhi

Copyright © 2017 by Joanne Fedler

Published in the United States by: Hay House, Inc.: www.hayhouse.com®
Published in Australia by: Hay House Australia Pty. Ltd.: www.hayhouse.com.au
Published in the United Kingdom by: Hay House UK, Ltd.: www.hayhouse.co.uk
Published in India by: Hay House Publishers India: www.hayhouse.co.in

Cover design: Amy Rose Grigoriou   Interior design: Alex Head

All rights reserved. No part of this book may be reproduced by any mechanical, photographic, or electronic process, or in the form of a phonographic recording; nor may it be stored in a retrieval system, transmitted, or otherwise be copied for public or private use—other than for "fair use" as brief quotations embodied in articles and reviews—without prior written permission of the publisher.

The author of this book does not dispense medical advice or prescribe the use of any technique as a form of treatment for physical, emotional, or medical problems without the advice of a physician, either directly or indirectly. The intent of the author is only to offer information of a general nature to help you in your quest for emotional, physical, and spiritual well-being. In the event you use any of the information in this book for yourself, the author and the publisher assume no responsibility for your actions.

Previously published in Australia by Joanne Fedler, ISBN 978-0-9954063-0-8.

Cataloging-in-Publication Data is on file at the Library of Congress

Tradepaper ISBN: 978-1-4019-5431-4

10 9 8 7 6 5 4 3 2 1
1st edition, July 2017

Printed in the United States of America

*This book is dedicated to all my students
who have shown me the way;
to everyone who longs to write but hasn't had the courage yet;
to anyone who's ever thought, "I have a story to tell";
to everyone brave enough to put feelings into words.
It's dedicated to you, my reader.
Write your story.
You never know whose life it might change.*

Whoever survives a test, whatever it may be,
must tell the story. That is his duty.

— Elie Wiesel, Holocaust survivor

You either walk inside your story and own it or
you stand outside your story and hustle for your worthiness.

— Brené Brown

Contents

A Note to the Writer

If you're anything like me, you've probably read way too many books on writing. Most of the time they keep us from doing the very thing we long for, the very reason we are reading a book on writing, which is to actually write. At the same time, as aspiring authors, we do need guidance. We want someone who's walked the path ahead of us to show us the way.

As with all life experiences, there's a fine balance each of us must strike between learning and doing, between research and forging our own path.

Over the past 12 years, I've been writing my own books and teaching others to write. I've written in just about every genre (except crime fiction and erotica), and what I've found is that no matter whether we're writing fiction or nonfiction, we cannot escape the fact that we're writing from our own self—the being who embodies the consciousness that compels us to write as well as the emotional history and sensuous existence from which we write. At the core of all great writing is a deep connection to the human heart. Even when we don't write *about* ourselves, we always write from our felt or imagined experience.

This book, then, is to help you find your way in to that beautiful, complex self and to value all it has felt, suffered, and known. Too many of us discount the victories and tragedies of our ordinary lives. We devalue our pain, we diminish our little loves. But truly, they are the source of any story we write.

This book is clearly for those of you who wish to write memoir, whether it's with a view to publication (traditional or self-publishing) or as a private record to leave a legacy for grandchildren. Or perhaps your words are just for you, and given that you're not one for public-restroom graffiti, writing your story is your way of telling the world, "I was here."

But it is also for those of you who want to explore the territories of your life and make sense of all you've experienced. What you'll discover in the writing and the remembering is that your life is rich with stories. And in those stories, you may find the seed of a fictional love story. The beginning of a murder mystery. The whisper of a dystopian young-adult novel.

As you begin, it's important to hold on to the hope that this book will be read by others. As the subtitle of this book indicates, this book will guide you to write your story so others will want to read it. This is not because I believe a book read only by its author is of necessity a sad little book that didn't get out much. I am not here to judge your book's karma. It's because writing for a reader is a discipline. It requires techniques I will share with you in this book. Even if you're the only one who ever reads your book, I invite you to treat yourself as your book's author first, and its reader second. And whether your book is read by others or not is irrelevant as long as you write it *as if* it is going to be read by readers. Chances are if you do, it will.

I have learned as much about writing from teaching and mentoring other writers as I have from writing my own books. This book, then, draws on my compassion for and love of all people who ache to write. I know you. Your fears, anxieties, doubts, and tremors. This book is intended to hold your hand and your heart through the stages of writing, from overcoming the thoughts that stop you, to the deep inner work of learning to trust yourself and the writing process, to offering you many ways into your story. Finally, I share "the how"—techniques I have developed over the years that I hope will demystify the writing process for you and break it down into manageable bits. If you've already read heaps of books on writing or taken writing courses, you'll find that some of my terminology is not a perfect fit with traditional writing ideas. I'm aware that when I use the term "transition" or "traveled," I'm imbuing it with my unique take. Originality is sometimes useful in teaching to avoid the dull echo of cliché and to help an idea click in a slightly different way. Stay with me on these. I am not intentionally setting out to confuse you. On the contrary, I want each idea to sprout bright and new for you.

In my many years as a writing mentor, I have found that 99 percent of what I do is not so much teach the craft of writing as hold the space for people as they begin to believe in themselves. I intend for this book to saturate you with as much as you may ever need to know about the craft of writing. But more than that, I hope it lifts you into the stories of your life with curiosity and sneaks courage into your pockets so you're able to write fearlessly and with conviction that who you are matters. Though we may never meet in person, we are energetically linked by the book you hold in your hands right now. And so, to the extent that I'm able to be with you in spirit as you read these pages, please know I hold this sacred space for you, and bless you on your writing journey.

Joanne Fedler

Part I

Thoughts

Be careful how you interpret the world. It is like that.

—Erich Heller

1

Everything is research

In the summer of 2001, I found myself sobbing into the phone. This was an evening ritual at around 5 P.M. when my two-year-old was throwing bits of mashed potato at me and my five-year-old was drawing on the walls of our rented home with colorful permanent markers. On the other end of the line was the strained, sad voice of my mum or dad, a link from another world, nine hours behind the life I was living. They would say kind things like, "It will get better," and "Take each day as it comes."

I was a new immigrant in Australia with two small kids. Lost and heartbroken about having left behind a life in which I'd been stitched into the fabric of friendship, kinship, and the security of knowing how things work and what things mean, I was clawing my way through each day. I was anxious about money. Schools. My physical and mental health. I found even the smallest tasks and routines overwhelming. It is a lonely business being bereft and inconsolable in ways that are inexplicable. Each night, my parents would phone to find out if I'd survived another day.

On one particularly bad evening, clutching the phone between my shoulder and neck while I wiped spaghetti off the carpet, I relayed some mundane cruelty from my day—receiving a parking ticket or being denied entry to the free story-time session at the local library because I hadn't prebooked tickets—my dad, a man with an artist's soul, said, "My darling, just take it one hour at a time. And pretend you're doing research for a book."

"What do you mean?" I sniffled.

"Someday," he said, "you'll look back on all this and see what great material it is to write about."

"A book?" I laughed. "Yeah, that'd be a bestseller, right?"

I had no idea how prophetic his words would turn out to be. But in that moment, something in me settled.

Material for a book. Somehow the burden of my life shifted a little. This was just a chapter in a story. A really shitty low point for a character involving carpet stains and grief. Maybe there was something in there.

2

The first review

Despite my dad's words of comfort, I had no cause to believe then that the dreary details of my day as a young mother on a temporary visa in Australia could interest anyone. Like, seriously?

Back then, there were many things I didn't understand. I had no concept of the deeply universal nature of all personal experience. At times I experienced my isolation as oxygen deprivation. I couldn't see further than the schedule for the next day, which—if it turned out to be a good one—would see me get the laundry done and a quick grocery run in. My life felt mistaken. Why had we left South Africa? Would I ever make a friend in Australia? Would I ever work again? Who was I, now that I was no one?

But years passed. I lived through the trauma. It found its right place. It became part of my story, winding through the fabric of my being. Oxygen returned. My son stopped throwing mashed potatoes and my daughter learned to draw on paper. I made friends. I made some serious heart-growing-back friends.

Three years later, I landed a book deal with an Australian publisher. Over the next few years I wrote and published three books, one about the hardships of early motherhood that went on to become an international bestseller. In Germany it outsold Harry Potter for a while.

Seven years after our arrival in Australia, I started working on a book about losing weight called *When Hungry, Eat*. Yeah, I know, riveting stuff. All stories need an "inciting event," and mine began with a visit to a dietitian who told me she wanted me to be "hungry." As I was writing the book, I realized there was a huge backstory, not to mention a subtext: I had started loading on the pounds after we immigrated. So I wrote about that. It became a cathartic way to process everything that had happened to me and my family. I wrote about how we had finally settled—we'd become Australian citizens, Zed and I had gotten married, and we'd made a sacred pilgrimage with our kids to Uluru, a massive sandstone monolith revered by Australia's indigenous people, to ask the ancient ancestral spirits for permission to settle here. (We bought a tourist package and stayed in a hotel, just so you understand there is no "epic tale" there.) As I wrote, I recovered. I felt my lost parts growing back. When I finished the book, my grief subsided.

In 2010, *When Hungry, Eat* was published. I'd never been so anxious about the release of a book, despite it being my fifth. I couldn't decide whether it was the most narcissistic, self-indulgent noise no one but my own mother would read, or whether it spoke to a universal story of displacement and making peace with change. Would I be ridiculed? Maligned on social media? Would anyone find anything of value in it? Would you have had to have mashed potatoes thrown at you to relate to it?

Waiting for reviews was excruciating.

And then the first one came out in the *Australian Bookseller and Publisher*.

It began: "Someone should canonize this book." It included phrases like "a golden nugget of autobiography, spiritual wisdom and health." My favorite sentence was "Think *Eat, Pray, Love* but less self-centred."

I cried when I read this. Someone had felt the pain of my silly little life with all its catastrophes. It was the final homecoming I'd needed.

Since *When Hungry, Eat* was published, I've received literally hundreds of e-mails such as these:

Thank you for writing your story. There were many parts of the book in which you could have been describing my life over the past 4 years—my feelings and experiences of immigration were so similar to yours. . . . I could totally relate to your descriptions of your feelings of loneliness, uselessness, depression, guilt, etc. I was either in fits of hysterical laughter (you are one very funny lady) or sobbing uncontrollably. The rawness of the emotions that you described so well really struck some chords in me and I felt like I had been through an intense therapy session at the end of every chapter. I really needed this book in my life right now and I thank you for that!
— M

Thank you for writing this incredible book! I had to put it down many times due to the flowing tears—so much of this could be my story. You have put into words what I have been unable to in the past 18 months since [immigrating]. Finally there is someone who can accurately and articulately describe how difficult it is to leave. . . . This book should be required reading for any new immigrant, even if just to show that they are not alone and that all the guilt, sadness, weight gain (I haven't yet met another immigrant who has not had this problem) and the feeling that you have lost your sense of self is normal.
— AW

Thanks for putting yourself on the line in your lines—it really gave me space to work through some of my own grief.
— A

And hundreds of e-mails expressing sentiments like these:

Your words have tremendous power and they will inspire generations.
— Sonya

You have put a lot of truth in that book.
— Patricia

And even one like this:

Since I start reading *When Hungry, Eat* I have been trying to give up smoking once and for all. Your book is an inspiration! As any smoker person I have tried going cold turkey . . . but in any odd situation . . . I'm back to the disgusting habit.
Hugs,
— M

How is it possible that a small story about such insignificant events could touch so many different people, and so profoundly?

3

Your story is never about you

Here's the first secret to writing your story: your story is never about you. It relates events and circumstances in your life and the emotional journey you've been on, but it is not about what happened to you. It's about how what happened to you can shed light on what happens to others. Your story is an echo of other stories. If you don't believe me, check out what Carl Jung and Joseph Campbell had to say about the universal consciousness that binds us all together. Go argue with them.

If we forget that we are part of a bigger story and fall into the narcissistic slumber of imagining that anyone outside of our immediate family is interested in the details of our lives, we will make the big mistake many aspiring authors do: believing we are celebrities and that people will be interested in us for no other reason than because we're cool or we've suffered.

In writing anything—but especially memoir—we must never forget that though we are writing *from* our story, we are writing *for* others.

The trick to writing memoir is to connect our own story to the interior story of the reader. Once we understand that our lives are smaller fractals, individual expressions of Life, it becomes easier to accept a) that our story is worthy and b) that others might find something valuable in our rendition of our experience.

One reader reviewed my book on Amazon like this:

> I wondered if it would only appeal to a narrow group of people who would be able to identify with this context. However, I soon realized that *it is a book about life, all our lives*, and facing the challenges life throws at us. Apart from merely being entertaining, I found the story inspiring and even potentially life changing with its profound insights.

So trust me when I say that your story, your perfectly distinctive life experience that is exclusive to you and you only, has resonance and relevance to other people. The trick, of course, is *how* you write it.

In this book I will share what I've learned about how to use the moments, anecdotes, funny little things that happen in our lives to write a rich, generous narrative that serves those who've taken time to read what we've written.

Your story has the power to change someone's life. Hell, if mine did, so could yours.

4

I know why
you're here

I know why you're here. You've got a form of hunger. A nagging itch.
Maybe it's jabbed you to put something down on paper. Or
it whines deep inside like a dogged tinnitus. It's what keeps you up
till 4 A.M. turning pages when you have an 8 A.M. meeting. It assails
you at odd, inconvenient moments. But no matter how little attention
you give it, it refuses to be banished or just die, goddamn it. So here
you are now.

The fact that you're reading this book means it's Serious. It is not
joking around. It's not going away. You can ignore it all you like. It's
calling you and has been for a long time. And if you don't do something about it, you're going to die with something unbirthed inside
you. Am I wrong?

What's brought you here is precious. Don't ever diss it or take it
for granted. It's your *longing*. And life would be a dismal trot between
meals and heartaches without it.

You know and I know that there's a Milky Way between longing
and its fulfillment. (Who doesn't long for a carnal encounter with a
Hemsworth brother or a lottery ticket made good?) But this is real life
and we are not delusional, even as we are still fervidly capable of hope

(we must be hopeful if we want to write). The truth is that until you actually write, the longing (like a good idea) stays frozen. No one but you will ever know of it, and certainly no one (not even you) will benefit from it. The only way for you to make that longing mean anything is to get words on the page.

So what transforms our longing to write our story into something more substantial than a corner in our hearts we visit occasionally?

I'm going to tell you in the pages that follow.

But first, let's deal with the clutter of objections that are getting in your way. Let's bury those bastards once and for all.

5

Here's why you haven't yet

I once posed naked for a photographer (when my body was still an advertisement for who I was), and trust me, a bit of flesh has nothing on writing.

When it comes to memoir, our terror of exposure and vulnerability is pornographically exaggerated. There is nowhere to hide—no fictional world, no imaginary universe. We assume that if our writing is rubbish, it must mean we are too. This fear of putting ourselves out there is the reason so many people—maybe even you—don't write their stories.

I conducted a survey among aspiring writers and asked, "What stops you from writing?"

People answered:

Lack of self-confidence that what I have to say matters.

Lack of belief that I will succeed.

Self-doubt, self-doubt, self-doubt.

Fear of not being good enough.

Do I have anything of value to say?

Fear that I am not a great writer.

I am worried that people will think the book is dreadful.

Fear of not being good enough.

I am scared to bare my soul.

Anxiety about the relevance and quality of the writing.

I don't believe in myself.

Geez, but it's a noisy marketplace of self-directed vitriol in there, isn't it?

And so, despite your longing, you haven't done it yet because:

- you don't know where or how to start;

- you're not a "real" writer;

- there are so many books out there, you wonder if it's worth it;

- you're not quite sure how to become a *New York Times* best-selling author;

- you don't know how to make your writing "clever" and fancy;

- you can't tell if your story will be interesting to others;

- you worry it's narcissistic and embarrassing to write about yourself;

- you're not sure if you have enough motivation to finish writing it (hell, you sometimes leave books half read);

- you wonder what people will think and say about you;

- it's not all happy stuff—maybe you should wait for your parents to die first;

- you don't know how to make it sound good—like, how do you use metaphor and shit?

- you don't have time to commit to writing something longer than a shopping list;

- you don't really believe you can;

- you're afraid of failure;

- you have no talent;

- you don't have what it takes to be a writer; or

- you don't know enough about writing and need to read this book first.

Let's line each of these objections up so we can get them out of the way.

6

Could someone just tell me where to start?

Living a life is a long and tedious business. Looked at this way, our story seems overwhelming. All the days we've lived, trips we've taken, people we've loved and lost, emotions we've felt . . .

So my advice is: don't take that long view. In fact, I want you to take the smallest snapshot of your life you possibly can.

The answer to the question "Where should I start?" is . . . anywhere. But as much as this is true, it is also unhelpful. "Anywhere" is too vast.

We need focus. In later sections in this book I will show you more than 100 triggers. There are many trails inward. But here's my point: it doesn't matter where you start. As long as you start small.

You do not need to—and please, please, for the sake of all of us, do not—write down every detail of your life since the day you were born. Because you'll write about that and realize you actually need to give some background on your mother, who was anxious, and possibly your father, who was out of work, and then maybe actually your grandmother and grandfather . . . It can go back thousands of generations before you've figured out where your story starts.

Where you *start writing* and where *your story begins* are two different things.

When it comes to the writing, just pick a day, a moment—any one at all will do. Writing happens in patches. It is haphazard. A bit here, a bit there. It's a random mulling, collecting, cherry-picking of memories: your eighth birthday when you got chicken pox under your eyelids. The day you waited for the school bus that never came. The night your dog Bobby got run over. That nightmare. That lover. That crush. A conversation with your dentist last Thursday about root canal. A fight you had with your mother about the pickled herring that had too much sugar in it. Find the tiniest scrap of memory, the teensiest moment you can access. Start writing there.

Then, much, much later in the process, when you have done enough random writing and have plenty of "bits," you will have to figure out what your story is and how to tell it. You will have to find a thread. You will have to do some big thinking and make narrative choices about where you want the reader to enter your story.

But not yet.

Your story will not be the rendition of your entire life, starting with your birth all the way to the present day. Memoir is a tapered, thematic snapshot of some significant part of your existence that sheds light on all human experience. And while it doesn't matter where your writing starts, it matters a whole big bloody deal where your "story" starts.

Maybe your story begins with the day you turned 45 and your wife left you and you realized you'd never known real love. Or the day your best friend was killed in a car accident and you decided to live life for both of you. Or the moment you were diagnosed with prostate or breast cancer and you went on a journey to heal your body and spirit. In *When Hungry, Eat*, I chose the day I visited a dietitian who told me I was obese (which inspired me to find a way to live with physical and emotional hunger).

Once you have decided where your story starts, you will then have to decide how to move your story from there. But what about what happened before that?

Ah, that's what backstory is for. That's where flashbacks are useful.

But first, you must write. So pick a place. Any place. A moment. Any moment. It is your provisional starting point. You can change your mind about where you want to structure your story later.

It doesn't matter where you start writing, just that you start.

7

Stop thinking, get writing

When I was a little girl, my dad, a brilliant cartoonist, would tell me and my sisters stories of princesses and dragons and castles. He would draw them for us and we would color them in. Watching him, I imagined I too could draw the imaginary worlds in my head— it looked so effortless. But as soon as I tried to get the images out of my head and onto paper, I was bewildered and disappointed.

That was when I stopped drawing.

The same thing happens to people with writing.

One way that we scare ourselves out of writing is that we take it so seriously. We want it to be perfect immediately. We start to feel a story inside us, and then as soon as we try to get it on the page, it comes out flat. Or we start and we realize that it's not coming out the way we want it to, so we stop and wait until we think we'll be more motivated or we'll know better how to do it. That's when paralysis sets in, because there's a voice inside us whispering, "This is crap."

If you want to write your story, you have to learn how to shut this voice up.

One way to silence it is to start freewriting.

Freewriting is writing that's done by hand (not on computers). Set your alarm for a period of time (5 to 20 minutes) and, using a writing prompt such as "I remember . . ." or "My mother always told me . . . ," keep your hand moving across the page until the alarm sounds. Don't stop to read what you've written. If nothing comes to mind from the prompt, just write the prompt over and over and over again until your time is up.

Another term for this practice is "dreamwriting." When we dream, we don't analyze what we're dreaming; associations come and go, bizarre scenarios appear before our eyes, and we participate in our dreams without stopping and saying, "This doesn't make sense."

We need to learn to write like we dream—freely and without inhibition.

If this sounds like a waste of time, it's not.

Here's why: when we sit down to write, there's a freight of unspoken pressure we've put on ourselves right then. There's so much at stake, we'd better write something worthwhile. It had better be bloody brilliant.

This is a flawless recipe for setting ourselves up to fail. The jabbering critics in our head overanalyze and criticize our thoughts as we transform them into writing. Sometimes they're so powerful they firehose us with self-doubt. To write authentically, we have to feel free. We have to loosen up our writing, like we would a muscle, so we don't cramp our own style.

Dreamwriting, then, is a way of short-circuiting the inner judge and setting the words inside you loose on the page.

We also cramp up with self-censorship because we imagine others reading what we've written.

But here's the thing with dreamwriting: no one is going to see it.

The most important rule of this kind of writing is that *you are free to write utter crap.*

Sometimes when you give yourself this freedom, you write a few gems in among the rubbish.

We also have to get used to writing stuff that we're happy to throw away. This teaches us to become less attached to the words we put on the page. The more unattached we are, the more we realize there's plenty where this came from. We develop an abundance mentality around our writing and prepare ourselves for the later task of editing, when we have to learn to let go of some of our writing.

The more we develop these skills, the more of a writer we become.

If we are precious and neurotic about every word we put on the page, sooner or later that is going to catch up with us. We will get verbally constipated. We'll develop writer's block. We will fail to cultivate the mental flexibility and resilience that writers need. The aim is: don't get stuck. Which is pretty good advice for how to live our lives in general.

8

But I'm not a "real writer"

As far as I'm aware, there's no body or institution that issues a certificate or degree that confers the title of "writer." It's not a nationality. You do not need a passport, or to pass a medical examination or even an English proficiency test. "Writer" is an identity you choose when you write. So start putting words on the page.

If you've never written before, that's okay. Everyone has to start somewhere. Your longing to write is a sign that this is something you're supposed to do. Before I was published, all I knew was that I wanted to write. The more I wrote, the better I got at it. Here are some signs that you should at least try:

- **You love "beautiful" writing:** You appreciate writing that is careful, sculptural. You re-read sentences sometimes because they're delicious. You sometimes read things aloud, to hear how they sound.

- **You underline or highlight words, sentences, or paragraphs in books:** You're not one of those "I don't mark up my books" people. You have no idea why you do this, except an inkling that someday you might want to come back to the places you've marked and re-experience those sentences. You detest e-books because you can't underline things with your pencil or make notes in the margins.

- **You like to eavesdrop on people's conversations:** Sitting in a café or at the bus stop, you listen in on conversations: teenage girls gossiping, spouses bickering, boys flirting, the banal and terrible stutterings and silences that happen between people. Writers are good listeners. We then imagine the stories behind the words. This is how we learn to write characters.

- **You love to people-watch:** You can sit and watch people go by for hours   the granny walking her wobbly poodle; the chubby guy resting his hand on his girlfriend's lower back; the rabbi in his black furry hat perspiring in the heat; the young mum with her whining toddler, talking on her mobile phone. Writers are keen observers—we look deeply, watching the rhythms and textures of all human interaction.

- **You notice the spaces around things:** You notice not only what people say and do, how they look and behave, but also what isn't there. The mother pushing the empty baby carriage. The pregnant woman without a wedding ring. The guy in the bar talking about his family. The newly renovated home that no one moves into. The car parked at the end of the road that never moves. Writers don't skim across the surface—we look in, around, through, and between things. We look for where stories hide.

- **You read books and think to yourself,** *Even I could write better than this***:** You get seriously irate when reading a badly written book. Sometimes you wonder, *How did this get published?* Being able to recognize what works and doesn't work means you're reading like a writer.

- **Sometimes words make you cry:** A sentence can bring tears to your eyes. Words move you.

- **You have empathy:** If you are naturally empathetic, you're able to imagine what it's like to be someone else—a person in a wheelchair, or someone who's homeless, kidnapped, raped, childless, lost . . . Writers imagine what it's like to be other people all the time.

Sometimes, all we have are these cues, nudging us in the direction of writing. So now that you know how to read those signs, catch them. Listen to them. Once you get a few words down, you can call yourself a writer.

Who's going to call you a liar?

9

Is it really worth it?

If you're asking, "Will I get published?" the answer is "There are no guarantees."

If you mean "Will I make money?" again, no assurances, and even if you do, it probably won't be much.

If you want to know "Will people read it?" who knows? We have little control over what happens to our writing when it goes out into the world (though we must be both strategic and proactive about finding an audience for our work).

If I said to you, "STOP WRITING NOW, for it may go nowhere. It may all just be a big fat waste of your time," would you?

If you would, then you should stop.

If you wouldn't, because you can't, then you're in it, my dear. You've got something growing inside you. And unless you want to abort it, tear it out of you like some misbegotten thing that doesn't yet have an answer to "How are you going to grow and who will you be when you come out?" then stop worrying about whether it's worth it.

If by asking if it's worth it you're asking, "Will I learn something valuable about myself? Will I create something beautiful? Will I create something worthy and of value?" the answers are YES, YES, and you'd better believe it, YES.

If "Is it worth it?" means "Is it worth finishing?" the answer is, of course, YES. Work hard. Make it beautiful. Let it shine with the time, effort, and energy you have invested in it.

That's what makes it worth it.

10

Who will care?

Your mother, I'm sure. If she's still alive, that is.

Some of your friends, maybe.

But mostly you.

What is painfully true is that the world is not waiting for our work. We are the only ones who know and care about it while it's in formation. We are its keeper, its incubator. If we lose it before we have birthed it, like a miscarriage, we are the only ones who will grieve its loss. No one else.

Our job is to make sure we write it right so that others will care when it comes into the world. If no one cares, we (and no one else) have failed to connect with our readers.

But don't get stuck. Start writing your next book.

11

How do I become a *New York Times* best-selling author? (and other distracting questions)

If this is your main objective in writing your story, my gentle suggestion is for you to let it go. At least for now. It's premature. To be a successful author, you have to be an author first. Which means you have to have finished a book.

Not everyone who wants to write a book can, or will.

Writing a book takes a certain kind of person, in the same way that climbing Kilimanjaro does. I am, for example, not the sort to summit a major mountain, being of anxious disposition, and I have no desire to risk death due to altitude sickness—I have a perfectly wonderful view from my study window. You need to find out if you are the kind of person who can write a book. And the only way to find out is to start writing.

It's easy to get too intimidated to write, or, at the other extreme, to think, *There's nothing to it*. Both are mistaken. It's hard, but it's not impossible. And you won't get anywhere without hard work, humility, and more hard work.

"Success" (however you choose to define it) doesn't flow automatically from knowledge of the writing process, mastery of the craft, and hard work. Maybe, then, we have to forget about success and just focus on the writing that's in front of us. Maybe, as the Holocaust survivor and author of *Man's Search for Meaning* Viktor Frankl reminds us, happiness cannot be chased. By living meaningful lives, happiness will flow indirectly to us.

So let's be sure you are pursuing what's "right" in writing. Which is:

a. getting started;

b. finding your authentic writing voice;

c. telling your story; and

d. finishing.

For now.

Once you've done that, then the work of getting the book out into the world begins. Other distracting questions you can shelve for now are: What font should I use on the cover? Where should I have my book launch? Let's leave those labors for another day, shall we? The best way to get something done is to begin.

12

My writing isn't clever or fancy enough

Would you go out on a date with someone who was "clever" and "fancy"? Nope, me neither.

Read John Steinbeck and you'll see that clean, plain language can be rich and textured when the thinking that accompanies it is clear and sophisticated. Writing is not—and should not be—"fancy." Whatever that means. We should write like we speak. Finding your writing voice has nothing to do with your vocabulary or grammar. Or spelling, for that matter. Once you're finished, you will have manuscript assessors, editors, and spell-check to help you smooth your story into shape for a reader.

If your vocabulary is atrocious and your grammar even worse, there's a great solution. Read. Write. Get feedback. This will magically improve your writing.

And by the way, if you don't read—please, please, don't write. You expect people to read and buy your book if you don't buy books, support authors, and read books yourself? Do you see the irony in that? Not to mention the karmic arrogance.

If you don't read but you have a great story to tell, start a podcast. A YouTube channel.

Leave the writing to people who care about books.

13

How can I tell if my story will be interesting enough to others?

Losing weight. Emigrating. Do these interest you much? I didn't think so.

It can be hard to tell if our stories will grab a reader.

While you're writing your story, you will believe on any given day that it is catatonia inducing. The next day you will know with utter certainty that it's as good as *Angela's Ashes*, maybe even better.

The truth is that it's not only the "what" of your story that makes it interesting. It's how you write it.

Just as the best joke can be slaughtered in the hands of someone with no sense of timing, so your story—as intriguing, scarring, and life changing as it was for you—must be told so that it lands for the reader.

Everything that follows in this book is about helping you get this part right so you don't end up talking just to yourself. And your mother.

There are two guiding questions when you write: "Who is this for?" and "Why would they care?" No book will be interesting to everyone. So choose your audience. Write for them. The clearer you are about who your book is for, the closer to their ears and hearts your writing will inch.

14

Isn't it narcissistic and embarrassing to write about myself?

I t's ironic that, despite our staggeringly narcissistic and self-promoting culture of curated Facebook profiles, we're terrified that writing about ourselves—honestly, vulnerably, and meaningfully—is cringe-worthy.

Still, gratuitous, untutored oversharing is not worthy of our readers' time and money. Our internal musings about our childhood, illness, divorce, dreams, or particular form of heartache will invariably bore and annoy readers unless we learn how to shape our writing to connect with them. More than in any other genre, writers of memoir need to keep our "so what?" wits about us. Our dull-o-meters need to be highly attuned.

We want to watch out for the dangers in writing memoir so we don't end up wallowing in the mud of our entire backstory. They are:

- writing in a voice that is too interior (musings, ruminations);

- including unnecessary and self-indulgent details that are interesting and important to us, but don't serve our story;

- not knowing what vision of the world our story is in service to;

- not understanding that we are writing for a reader (and who that reader is);

- not including enough action;

- not creating compelling "characters" (including ourselves);

- not creating an interesting story structure;

- mistaking what to reveal and what not to reveal; and

- not understanding what a story is and how ours must follow the arc of storytelling.

And most important, we must make the "transition" from the personal to the universal. I deal with this in detail in later chapters.

15

Somebody's already written what I want to write

No, they haven't.

No one can write your story the way you can. You are the only one who can tell your story. Your life experiences and sensibility are what make your writing unique, not simply what happened to you

In the words of writer Mary Gaitskill:

> Writing is . . . being able to take something whole and fiercely alive that exists inside you in some unknowable combination of thought, feeling, physicality, and spirit, and to then store it like a genie in tense, tiny black symbols on a calm white page.

Not to get all Barney the dinosaur on you, but there is no one who has the precise combination of lived moments, feeling, and intelligence as you. Your heart's shape is as distinctive as your fingerprint. You *are* special.

Nobody can write the story you have to tell the way you can.

16

What if I don't finish?

You'll never know unless you start. Finishing happens after starting. So focus on the first steps first.

17

I've been writing for a while, but now it's gotten too hard

The middle is not the glory zone. But is it ever? Mid-labor? Mid-life?

I saw this on Facebook recently:

Three Stages of Life

Birth

WHAT THE FUCK IS THIS?

Death

Writing's a lot like this. It gets hard. There's only one way, and that's through. My hope is that this book will help you work your way through the "too hard" stage and to the finish line.

18

What will people think and say?

If I'm in a particularly self-torturing mood, I simply head over to Amazon and browse some of the one-star reviews of my books. There may be 50 five-star reviews, but it's the stingy ones I remember. I did this a lot as a young author. It did not add sunshine to my life.

So, I've developed a 100 percent effective method for dealing with what others think and say about me. I learned this trick many years ago when I was traveling through Malawi with a boyfriend. We met a young man named Binos whom we paid to take us out on Lake Malawi in a dugout, a type of boat that's a hollowed-out tree trunk. On the side of the dugout were carved the words "Let Them Say." We asked Binos what that meant. He explained that people in Malawi subsist by fishing. To be a successful fisherman, one needs a dugout. To buy a tree from the Malawian government costs a lot of money. Those Malawians rich enough to buy a tree know that behind their backs, people will say, "That man is rich."

Let them say.

We have no control over what others will think or say about us once our work is out in the world. Worrying about it is a waste of precious writing and creative time and will only sabotage our efforts to keep writing. I've just chosen not to hang with that kind of crowd anymore.

What will people say? Who knows? Maybe nothing. Maybe they'll trash-talk about us, in private or in public. What others think and say about us is none of our business. I create. Others criticize. I choose to be on the side of creation. There are always trolls and haters in the world. But I am too busy creating to be a troll tamer. And so should you be.

Let them say.

19

Should I wait for my parents to die?

Another reason you may not have written your story yet is because basically you're a nice person. You don't want to hurt your kids, your ex, or other family members who are implicated in the story, especially if your story is a hard one—abuse, addiction, gambling, drugs, murder, suicide, psychological damage. I get it. This is a tough one.

Every family has secrets. We all have tales of horror tucked away in our past. Sometimes these stories aren't even ours to tell; maybe your grandmother was a Holocaust survivor, or your best friend was raped, or your brother was a drug addict. You may feel that although you were shaped, scarred, even mangled by these circumstances, you were just a witness.

But your story as a witness is interesting and valid. It is a particular point of view that deserves a telling.

Nevertheless, you may still need to think carefully about how you approach this.

Some solutions:

- Ask permission of the family member to tell their story.
  I have done this with many of my books (*Secret Mothers' Business*; *When Hungry, Eat*; and *Love in the Time of*

Contempt), knowing that if someone said no, I just wouldn't use their story.

- Write a similar kind of story, but change important facts, working thematically rather than factually (as I did in my book *Things without a Name*).

- Use a pseudonym if it is published.

- Change details to protect the identity of certain family members.

- Write your life story as fiction or fictionalize parts of it and alert the reader up front by saying something like "based on a true story" or "largely based on events that took place."

I suspect that sometimes we use not wanting to hurt other people as an excuse for not writing. Fine, if that's where you are, move on. Write science fiction. Erotica. Crime thrillers.

But don't confuse writing your story with getting published. Once you have a completed manuscript, you can start to think about ways of sharing your story that are safe, legal, palatable, and manageable for you. There's a big difference between what you bare on the page and what you share. You cannot make sharing decisions until you have done all the baring first. If you don't get that part done, you don't have to worry about sharing. You need to pour it all out before you pare it all back. Think about the right things at the right times. Don't preempt, assume, or imagine a future that isn't here yet.

So it comes down to this: you can bide your time and wait for family members to die, or you can write your story anyway and trust that you will figure out the problem of how to share it later on.

20

Do I need to use metaphor and shit?

You don't have to use metaphor, simile, personification, or any other narrative flourishes. But you do need to work the craft. Author Malcolm Gladwell put a number on it—he said that to become an expert at anything, you need to devote roughly 10,000 hours to the task.

I guess that weeds out those of us who were hoping for a shortcut.

Some of us think that somehow we will escape having to do the time, because we're talented and we're the exception to the rule.

This may be the case for a lucky few, but for the rest of us schmucks, there's only one way to get to where we want to get to—and that's by learning our craft conscientiously.

Ira Glass, the American radio personality and host of *This American Life*, said that when we begin creative work, no one ever tells us that there is "a gap" between our "taste" and our output. What we create has potential, but it's "just not that good." The reason we're so disappointed is because we actually have good taste and we know we're not quite there. Right here is where many people quit. They don't know how to push through. But the only way to close the gap is to keep creating and refining.

Writers who succeed know that there is a craft that has to be learned, and they learn that craft diligently. No matter how brilliant or compelling our story is, we have to find ways of writing it so we can share what is implicit and subtle in our experience so it connects with others. We do this by making conscious narrative decisions.

We may instinctively know that a protagonist or narrator needs to change from the beginning of a story to the end of the story, but do we understand why? And are there ways of structuring our story more intentionally to create a more enriching experience for the reader? We may know that short, sharp sentences are better than long-winded ones laden with adjectives and adverbs, but do we understand how to implement this in our own writing?

If this sounds nerdy, become a nerd. There's much to learn about how to write well, how to improve your writing, and what makes writing powerful.

Learning the craft will help you figure out:

- where you are in the writing process;

- the basics of good storytelling (how to structure a story);

- how to create fascinating, complex characters your reader will care about;

- how to write great dialogue;

- the difference between plot and structure;

- what point of view is and why it matters;

- the pros and cons of using a first- or third-person narrator;

- the difference between showing and telling and when to use each;

- what is unique about the genre you're working in—in this case, memoir;

- what your story is about, what the "concept" is;

- what your themes are and how to enrich your text with them;

- how to improve your language;

- how to eliminate cliché;

- how to decide what to include and what not to include;

- how to get your writing to shine, sparkle, and shimmer with your individual take on the world;

- how to take an abstract idea and make it tangible, sensual, human; and

- how to take a concrete idea and give it texture, color, and depth by finding abstract themes, images, metaphors, and paradoxes.

There are hundreds of fabulous books written to help you get a grip on the mechanics of writing, and an appendix at the back of this book lists some of the best ones that have helped me. Study the craft. Learn what you need to know. It will empower you.

21

I don't have time

There are things we all want in life—to lose weight, live a healthier life, meditate more, be kinder, spend more time with our kids, make an effort to see friends, be tidier, or meet our soul mate. There's only one thing that stands in our way: what we are prepared to do to get there. Only when we take ACTION do our "wants" turn a corner. They change alchemically from heart fluff into heart muscle. They solidify. The universe has to accord them gravity and space and to take notice of them.

Imagine if you were told that by writing every day for a year, you would cure a life-threatening condition, ensure the safety of your child, or save the planet. You'd find the time.

Look, I'm all for hobbies—we all need something to do with our spare time when we're not working or engaged in the gazillion *should*s, *must*s, and *have-to*s of our lives. Scrapbooking, knitting, practicing the ukulele. I'm a great fan of puttering. I can while away entire days just dabbling in this and that.

But if writing is just a hobby, chances are it will remain hobby-zoned.

Writing was just a hobby for me for 10 years. I used to write at night after work—sometimes, when I felt like it or I felt motivated. And I'd attend a weekly writers' group. When my kids were little,

Zed would take them out on a Sunday morning and give me a few hours to "potter" on my writing. But 10 years later, when I was at a dead end in my professional life, Zed said to me, "You are a miserable wretch. Why don't you finish that bloody book you've been writing for ten years?"

"I won't be able to earn any money for a while," I sniffled.

"We can survive," he said. "Baked beans on toast for a few months doesn't sound so bad."

Only when he gave me this permission did I knuckle down, and for six months I focused entirely on pulling my novel together.

There are professors who work full-time who manage to write books. Waitresses who work double shifts. They wake in the dark to get two hours of writing done before their day begins. They write on weekends. They sacrifice. A book gathers momentum, the blade of its message becomes sharpened, its coherence sets when we dedicate ourselves to it. Even if we can only devote part-time hours to it, we can devote full-time attention to it.

Without this kind of commitment, we're just puttering.

So, you want to write?

Steal time.

Make time.

Sneak time.

Take time.

No one gives it to you.

Or just don't write.

The only person you will make miserable is you.

22

I don't really believe I can do this

Some of us are born thinking we're superstars (predominantly those of us with Jewish parents, like me).

The rest of us earn our self-worth by testing our dreams against the world. If we're robust, we return after failure and try again. And again, each time a little more robust and resilient. But I know few people (barring the megalomaniacs) who are spared the tilt around the anxiety of "Am I up to this?" or "Who am I to have these wild and wicked dreams?" Some of us manage the wobble better than others. Some of us are more practiced at finding the center. But trust me, we're all tuned in to the silent whine in our inner ear of "Can I really pull this off?"

If you give too much attention to resistance, it will block you from writing like a brutal bouncer at the door of a club you want entry to. So you have to be smart. Brave. Unflinching. Make creative choices.

One of my favorite quotes by the poet Robert Frost hangs above my desk:

You're always believing ahead of your evidence.

What was the evidence I could write a poem?

I just believed it.

The most creative thing in us is to believe in a thing.

It's the poetic equivalent of Nike's Just Do It. Frost is saying that believing in yourself is a choice. It's up to you. Self-belief is not a fact, it's an attitude, and we measure it based not on who we are, but on what we do. Sitting around wishing we could write will not build our self-belief. But writing something—even if it needs a lot of work—will give us a sense of accomplishment. With feedback and work we can improve it, and then we will think, *This isn't so bad,* and maybe even, *Huh, I wrote that? It's pretty good.*

And voilà, suddenly you believe.

23

I'm afraid of failure

Funny that.

Do you think there's anybody who's not? We all are, just as we all fear rejection and dying. No one gets a free pass on this one. So seriously, suck it up. If you weren't afraid, you'd be insufferable. Writers are always doing the dance between "just believe" and "fear failure." That's what makes our efforts worth it—that we have battled with ourselves and spilled blood on the page and we have words to show for it. Get used to having that fear hanging around in the same way you have to learn to live with migraines or a neighbor with a yappy dog. If we can't eliminate them, we learn how to manage them. We work around them.

But if fear stops us from writing, we've given it far too much power. It's become the boss of us. We have to wrestle it into submission—or lock it in the basement for a few hours—so we can write.

I know you want a guarantee. You want someone to underwrite your investment of time, energy, money, and love and make promises that if you do everything right, you'll finish your book, it will be brilliant, you'll have publishers fighting over you, and you'll go on to become J. K. Rowling, rich and famous.

But I can't give you that, because:

a. I'm not God;

b. there are no guarantees in life, ever; and

c. the truth is, it's unlikely to happen.

Failure is part of what makes life interesting. So go ahead, and if you fail, remember—you're just "doing research for a book."

Besides, a completed manuscript—even one that is unpublished and has been rejected by publishers a million times—is only a failure if that's the title you've chosen for it. I prefer "bloody well finished."

24

I have no talent

Who gets to legislate who has talent and who has none? Your primary school teacher who screeched and carved red lines through your work?

I had one of those. Her name was Ms. Richards, and I was 11. She detested me for no reason I could ever work out. She had her favorites and I was not one of them. But I figured out early on that I didn't want her as a passenger on my tour bus. I left her in my fourth-grade classroom. She was a sad and bitter human being, and what she thought of my talent was never going to determine my future behavior and success.

On the other hand, my tenth-grade teacher, Mrs. Orkin, loved my writing. I carry her in my heart with every book I write. Find people who love what you do and want to hear your story. Then write about your own Ms. Richards—these folks make great characters in our books.

And we get to exact long-overdue revenge.

25

An aside on talent for the tragically untalented

H ere's what I think about "talent."

Talent isn't enough: Some of us, it's true, have an innate flair for writing. So we imagine, *I've got this.* We act like we've got a business-class ticket. But we don't. Talent is not even our boarding pass. It may get a writer to the terminal, but it does not guarantee takeoff, a smooth journey, or arrival at any given destination. Getting to where we want to go is, perhaps counterintuitively, unconnected with talent. (It has far more to do with stamina.) *Talent* is who you are. *Stamina* is what you do. Blissfully untalented writers can have Fifty Shades of commercial success because they have muscle in places "talented" writers neglect.

Talent often tags along with debilitating neurosis: Gifted writers can be serious nutcases. (I say this with great affection—any one of us might be a slight nutcase.) They are blessed with a form of self-consciousness that, although it is a writing strength (it makes their writing glimmer with depth and takes a reader into some of the most hard-to-reach internal spaces), when turned on itself, can be paralyzing. They overanalyze and overthink what others will say. They become hunchbacked with self-doubt and shattering vulnerability. They often self-sabotage. They don't write. They struggle to finish.

Talent gives people a false sense of entitlement: Just because someone has talent, it doesn't make them special (remember, we're all special). I know, I'm sorry, this must come as terrible news to the talented. We all nurture the romantic fantasy of being discovered, based on one or two fairy-tale success stories of famous writers who became multimillionaires overnight. If this is your Plan A, my quiet suggestion is to put a Plan B in place (one that does not rely on the same elements that produce a lottery win). No matter how gifted a writer you might be, we are all subject to the same rules of the game: hard work, perseverance, and the willingness to refine our craft. Talent is not a shortcut, although it might give you a head start in the confidence department. Tortoises can beat hares.

If you were born with writing talent, you're one of the lucky ones. If you believe you have none, please don't stop reading this book. If you have something to say, I will teach you how to harness the qualities you already possess to start, write, and finish what is burning inside you.

26

I just don't think I have what it takes to be a writer

What does it take? Is there like a checklist?

When we start anything new, we're going to come up against stuff we can't do yet. Because we're beginners. When we start writing, we're often:

- turning out writing that's clichéd, sentimental, and unoriginal;
- uncertain about our own abilities;
- short on experience as writers (we haven't spent enough time on the craft);
- far from our authentic writing voice and scared to take risks;
- not really in tune with why we're writing or who it's for; or
- impatient and give up too easily.

But all of these can be overcome. We simply need to develop certain qualities to help us work through these challenges. To overcome lack of originality, we need to cultivate **curiosity**; to forge through self-doubt, we need to foster **conviction**; if we're inexperienced and haven't done our homework, we need to buckle down **conscientiously** and do the work; to get to our writing voice, we will need to take risks, and that will take fastidious **courage**. In writing to reach an audience, we need to be **connected** to our story and to the bigger story we are sharing with our readers. And if we are going to finish what we started, we need **commitment**.

What you'll notice is that these states of being have less to do with writing and more to do with *the writer*. If we don't possess these qualities innately, we can learn them. They begin with our thinking. If we can change our thoughts, we can develop any number of new qualities.

Writing, we are taught, is character driven.

Not only those in our stories. I'm talking about you, the writer.

Yep, you're driving.

27

I need to read
this book first

The question you should be asking yourself right now is whether reading this book is your own personal form of procrastination or resistance. You could read endlessly about how to write without ever actually writing. If you really want to write, shouldn't you toss this book aside and get some words down?

When we start writing, we imagine that there's a secret, maybe even The Secret, that we have been too thick to unearth unassisted and that, once learned, will ignite the fires of our own creativity. Like addicts, we tell ourselves, *Just one more book. One more writing exercise that begins, "I remember . . ." One more instructive "Show, don't tell."* Sometimes, we're readily distracted by promises of iridescent "it's-out-there-somewheres."

Reading is no substitute for doing. Self-help feeds on self-doubt.

So you can read this book. But after you've read it, you have to promise yourself that you're going to write your own.

28

Yes, you should,
and here's why

Let's forget about "them" for a while.

They can get in the way. The publishers, the readers, the reviewers—all those who are not sitting at your desk trying to get words onto the page. "They" who may never materialize, but who haunt you nonetheless.

Start by writing for the most important person, the only one who counts. Write for you.

Markus Zusak, author of *The Book Thief*, said in an interview, "I set out to write a book that meant something to me, but I ended up writing a book that means everything to me. That's probably the first reason it has had any success at all, let alone international success. . . . As a reader there is something about encountering a book when you have a sense that it means a great deal to the author."

So write what you care deeply about. Get clear on why you are writing. Don't do it from your ego—think bigger: what does my story offer to someone else? Don't be pretentious or grandiose. Readers see through posturing. And we will eventually get tired of our own posturing too.

Think of writing about your life as a pilgrimage, a search for personal and emotional truth. Guided by the lantern of language, you will learn to see, know, and understand yourself better. The poet Mary Oliver writes in "Sometimes" from her collection of poetry *Red Bird* that to live a life we must be able to do three things: bring our full attention, allow ourselves to be astonished, and then relay what we've witnessed.

When we give our own lives attention, they become illuminated. As we write our journey, we mark our heart's trail, and map our internal territory: *I was innocent . . . I was loved . . . I was lost . . . I was broken . . . I found joy. . . .* We name the nameless. We come softly upon insights. And because we now know the truth, we can choose our self-disclosure. The only person you owe anything to is yourself.

I hope by now some of the reasons you can't write have loosened their hold on you. In the chapters that follow I am going to introduce you to every good reason why you should give everything you have to your writing.

29

Write to meet yourself

Oscar Wilde famously said, "Most people are other people. Their thoughts are someone else's opinions, their lives a mimicry, their passions a quotation." In lives bombarded by media and op-ed and news we have no part in creating, we flail about in roles, social constructs, ideologies, privileges, and philosophies that are so invisible and infectious, we're completely unaware of whether we actually believe them or want them as part of our story.

I woke up to this in my early 20s when I realized that although I was expected to love live concerts and clubs, I detested them. For a long time I pretended to enjoy them, because I wanted to fit in. I dragged myself to smoky, noisy, disco-ball, epilepsy-inducing, light-flickering, eardrum-damaging clubs, drank alcohol I didn't want, and tried to be sexy. I invariably came home with terrible stomach cramps. When I owned the fact that I actually detest crowds, noise, and disco balls, I felt my spirit chiropractically align. I became myself.

Sometimes we fall in with the pack because we don't want to seem difficult. We want people to like us. And we don't want to miss out on "the fun" that everyone is having. But what's fun for some is not fun for everyone, and I have come to the place in my life where I want to choose what's fun for me, even if it involves five days of silent meditation (which to my husband sounds like hell). Likewise, flying to New York to run a marathon would be a form of torture for me, but it gives him joy and meaning.

Each time we claim a piece of ourselves through our preferences and our non-negotiables, we fortify our spirit. We lay a cable through the architecture of our beings. We wake up from the dream walk of following the crowd, walking someone else's path, living out someone else's expectations for our lives.

When we write our story, we confirm *I prefer this to that. I belong to my history, to my family, to my past, to my memories.* For those of us who feel lost, writing our story grounds us in a firm sense of conscious selfhood.

30

Write to break the silence

Words came easily to me.

Apparently I started speaking when I was nine months old. My older sister, Carolyn, was born deaf and couldn't speak. She and I had a special bond that required no language. I was the only one who could understand her. So at nine months, by all accounts, I became her interpreter.

As a child, when our family crowded around the TV to watch *Bonanza* or *Little House on the Prairie,* I'd watch, then turn to Carolyn and silently mouth the key plot points. I learned to summarize and to pick out what was important.

I watched my sister go through 12 grueling years of speech and hearing therapy to learn to pronounce her *s*'s and *th*'s so she could make herself understood in the world.

When something comes easily, like language did for me, it's natural to take it for granted. When we have never had to struggle or reach for something, we imagine it is our birthright. We don't see it for what it is. Health works that way. Food on the table. The right to vote. Freedom from violence. Instead, I have always felt how precious words are. How some have to struggle for them. How painstaking it can be for some to find their voice. And I have always felt, as one who has a voice, an overwhelming responsibility to use my words well and wisely and to speak up on behalf of those who cannot speak for themselves.

Many of us can speak. But we have no voice. We don't speak what is true—perhaps we don't even know what is true for ourselves. When we undertake to write our journey, we are committing to breaking a silence within us, to discovering who we really are. Words become bridges. Without words and language, we have no voice. We are cut off. Alone. Writing connects us inward and to each other, so that we can belong to our own true selves and to this world.

When we can put something into language, when we can give shape to our shames and shadows, they transmute, they get sucked like a dark genie back into the magic lamp of language, where we can contain them.

31

Write to take back your power

To tell a story, we must believe that we have a right to tell it. For those of us who feel powerless, writing our stories helps us reclaim our power. We get to remember events in the way that we experienced them—not factually, but emotionally. We get to call "the incident" "rape," or "incest." We choose what we call ourselves: a "survivor," rather than a "victim"; a "woman who loved her children and stayed," rather than a "battered woman."

My novel *Things without a Name* begins like this:

Nonna taught me how to read. My first book was made of cardboard and had pictures with words next to them. Nonna pointed at the letters next to a picture of a house. H-OU-Z. She pointed at the letters alongside a bird. B-I-R-T. Because she has a thick Italian accent, I learned to read English with an Italian accent. "NONNA—is me. FAITH—is you. Everywhere you look, up, down, here, there, things have a name."

"Why must things have names?" I asked.

"Otherwise how must we know what it is? Things need names for onderstanding. So if you ask for *fiore*, a flower, I don't bring you *ragno*, a spider." And she wiggled her nine fingers like a spider's legs.

"But I like spiders," I told Nonna.

"Yes, but a spider is not a flower."

"What about things that don't have names?" I asked. "Like the colour of yesterday and the things we forget."

Nonna lifted her four-fingered hand to her mouth like she was holding a truth from slipping out. She smiled briefly before she answered me:

"They don't exist. And if they do, they are *dimenticato*. Lost."

That book was about finding names for things inside ourselves so we can claim our power and love ourselves back into being.

When we write our own story and name things for ourselves, we find moments of our strength, when the narrative we've inherited has been that we were weak. We describe the exact textures of our suffering when we've been labeled a troublemaker or a loser. In writing, we get to choose our words. We get to name ourselves.

We literally get to rewrite history.

32

Write to make meaning

The past is often a chaotic fog of events we never fully understood or processed. When we write a story, we create an ordered pattern out of those events, and so structure meaning.

Stories follow a deep structure that is almost encoded in the human brain—or maybe the heart. When we start to put the puzzle together, we begin to see the way in which it all holds itself together.

As humans, we're hardwired to make meaning out of things. Meaning is not inherent in an experience, as Viktor Frankl taught in logotherapy, a psychotherapeutic approach based on the belief that human nature is motivated by the search for a life purpose. The pursuit of meaning is an act of creativity on our part, in each moment of our lives.

Isn't that an exciting thought?

33

Write to heal

One of the questions Native Americans ask sick people is "When last did you tell your story?"

Dr. Lewis Mehl-Madrona (a wonderful physician and author of *Narrative Medicine*) uses storytelling to help people heal from physical and mental illness. He asks them to tell the story of their illness and to claim a different narrative: "Change the story and the illness may change."

Sometimes words are our only freedom. They liberate us from ourselves. From past painful experience. From numbness. From wounds that have no names.

The writer Maxine Hong Kingston helps Vietnam veterans write their stories, which in turn helps them heal from the trauma. Stories work in mysterious ways on the brain and engage the mind, heart, and spirit in a mystical conversation that can bring peace to injured places.

It took me two years to write *When Hungry, Eat*. There were times when writing was so painful, I literally couldn't see the screen in front of me for my tears. In one particular scene, I am trying to say good-bye to my friend Ilze. I wrote and rewrote that passage maybe a hundred times, until I could write it without crying. By the time I finished it, all my grief at our good-bye was stitched into a few short, unsentimental sentences. Writing that book helped me to hold my loss.

In owning our stories, we magically, paradoxically, are able to let them go. That's the deal the Muse has struck with Life. Own it. Really own it. And it will let you leave without the pain.

34

Write to bear witness

Anne Frank wrote in her diaries:

> Unless you write yourself, you can't know how wonderful it is. . . .
> And if I don't have the talent to write books or newspaper articles,
> I can always write for myself. . . . When I write I can shake off all
> my cares. My sorrow disappears, my spirits are revived! . . . Writing
> allows me to record everything, all my thoughts, ideals and fantasies.

For those of us who have never been listened to or had anyone bear witness to our suffering, writing our story can be a beautiful experience of self-acknowledgment.

It is our way of saying, "I was here."

35

Write to remember

You may not think you remember much about your childhood. But when you start to write, doors open where before there were just long corridors of time that had passed. You begin to remember more. You locate the joy, the grief, the abandonment, the emotional experience that defined you. But how do you know if a memory is worth writing about? As the wonderful writing teacher Julia Cameron puts It, "If a memory is strong for you, trust it . . . If an incident has weight for you, then it is significant. Trust yourself in this. . . . The audience we require is our own loving attention."

When we write, our brains (or hearts or heart-minds) efficiently cluster information together so that our consciousness can access larger chunks, and we're able to more easily recall details and store our memories. We collect bits of ourselves we have left behind, we become more integrated and whole as we make peace with our shadow energies and lost stories.

Memoir is as much about the nature of memory as it is about "what happened to me." In fact, memoir is an investigation of the way in which memory works: memory is unreliable, powerful, and can confuse and conflate events.

Memory is a foundation of our identity. When we remember things that have happened, we own our histories.

36

Write to meet
yourself . . . again

Our lives come at us with vicious speed. We're endlessly "doing" and "keeping up," which is why many of us feel like we're always lagging behind. One day we may wonder, *Is this it?* and *What's it all about?*

In the rush, we've lost an intimacy with and curiosity about ourselves. This breakdown of self-worth is evident when we feel no passion or sense of purpose about anything. So the very act of writing our story is welcoming self-compassion and curiosity back into our lives. We cannot help but grow and transform through this slow, patient, probing engagement with our inner world. Writing is a profound act of intimacy and curiosity with our own consciousness.

In re-meeting ourselves on the page over and over again, we learn to love this broken, stumbling self. We learn to have compassion. And thus we embody the exquisite line from Galway Kinnell's poem "Saint Francis and the Sow": "Sometimes it is necessary to reteach a thing its loveliness."

Write to reteach yourself whatever it is you need to know.

37

Write to tell the truth

Julia Cameron writes in her book *The Right to Write* that honesty is an important aspect of the writing process. "Faced on the page, a difficult truth becomes a doorway."

We often choose not to know what we know, but when we write, the truth offers itself to us. We cannot pretend *I am happy*, or *This is enough of a life for me*. When we write, we enter the darkness of our deepest selves, and as we write, our words become eyes that adjust, making out the shapes in the shadows—the armchair of our self-loathing, the piano of our pain. We stumble over the litter of our grief.

We get better at seeing into these unlit places.

38

Write to connect

Though we might write for ourselves, a story implies that there is a teller and a listener—it is created for the purpose of sharing meaning. Stories help us connect with others and create relationships. Words rescue us from catastrophic loneliness and remind us that we are part of the great family of humanity.

For those of us who feel alone, our stories act as bridges to others and build community.

39

Your book could change someone's life

We have all read books that have shifted our emotions or thoughts so much that we were altered when we finished them.

Not all books that change our lives deal with dramatic events. Sometimes it's the author's ability to find humor in difficulty that moves us. Or the depiction of a kind interaction that inspires us to think about how we speak to our partners. Or a tale of a trip undertaken that motivates us to get off our arses and go someplace new.

As readers, we're inspired by true stories where authors share their experiences and reflect on what they've been through. Because of their struggle, we're able to look at our own lives in a different way.

So here is another clue: in order for our story to reach others, we're not just recording the events of our life and obsessively recalling the details about where our mother was born, what trade our great-grandfather was involved in, and what town our grandmother came from.

We're taking readers on an emotional journey. Feelings matter more than facts.

Here are some of the books that have changed my life (many of which are memoirs):

- *How to Be Sick*, by Toni Bernhard, is a book by an author with such a severe chronic illness that she cannot sit or speak for long periods. Written from a Buddhist perspective, she shows how even in the bleakest of circumstances we can redeem our experiences by seeing them as teaching moments. It has transformed how I think of my own frailties and given me patience with slipped disks, back pain, and plantar fasciitis. It is one of the most profound ruminations on impermanence and mortality.

- *Man's Search for Meaning* by Viktor Frankl. This gave me a completely new framework for experiencing the world. I used to believe I had to "find" meaning. Now I approach life as a creator—I make meaning.

- *Why People Don't Heal and How They Can* by Caroline Myss. This helped me understand the connections between the body, mind, and spirit. When I had a cancer scare some years ago, this book became my guide and companion and allowed me to let go of the emotional pain I was holding. I refer to it whenever I have a physical symptom and am trying to understand its emotional counterpart.

- *Teach Us to Sit Still* by Tim Parks. This inspired me to think beyond conventional Western medicine when it comes to finding cures for physical conditions and not to trust my own skepticism. It has opened me to the mysteries of healing.

- *Boy*, by Kate Shand, tells of Kate's attempt to understand why her 14-year-old son, JP, committed suicide. She examines her own parenting unflinchingly to find out how she failed and where, if anywhere, her guilt lies. This book made me think more carefully about how I parent my children. I began to pay attention to their emotional worlds. I came away from reading it with a deep understanding that our job as parents is to stay connected to our kids, and to accept that, no matter what we do, they have their sovereign paths to live. Loving a child is about letting them go.

- *The Still Point of the Turning World* by Emily Rapp. Emily learns when her son Ronan is just nine months old that he has Tay-Sachs disease, a degenerative condition that claims the lives of all those who have it by the age of three. This book is Emily's attempt to come to terms with loving a child who has no future. It is a deep and searing examination of love and grief. I read it after my friend Emma died suddenly at the age of 35. I cannot tell you what comfort this book gave me, just to be in the company of someone who was holding raw grief in such a conscious, meaningful way.

- *Wave* by Sonali Deraniyagala. This is one of the hardest books I've ever read. It's about the author's unimaginable experience of losing both of her young sons, her husband, and her parents in the tsunami in Sri Lanka in 2004. She writes without sentimentality or self-pity, but simply to come to terms with who she is now. I always imagined a human being would literally die in the face of such loss. And Sonali nearly did. She was on suicide watch for a long time. But she gasped her way through to write this book. She battles with coming to terms with her lone survival and how she will continue to be a human being. I came away overwhelmed with gratitude for the simple wholeness of my family and the domestic intactness of my own life.

- *Bird by Bird* by Anne Lamott. This is a joyous, honest, self-deprecating book about writing. I read it when I was a young writer, and it gave me such comfort to know that my own fears and anxieties were shared by someone as accomplished as the author. It is a book I still refer to 20 years later, and it has formed the foundation of how I think about and teach others how to write.

I could go on and on . . . but you get my point.

So, think about which books have changed your life and the gratitude you feel to their authors for writing them.

Someday, someone could feel just that way about yours.

40

What's a story?

A story is not just about what happened when and to whom. To make a reader care, we have to create an emotional connection. This is the essence of storytelling.

So what, then, is a story?

These are some of the elements:

- Once upon a time there was a fascinating, sympathetic character

- who lived in a particular world (a time and a place)

- and this character wanted something

- that she or he could not have because of all kinds of conflicts and obstacles

- but she or he overcame them

- and was transformed in the process.

Ultimately, a story has to move us from point A to point B—and something has to change in either the character or the reader.

Over the years, I've seen a lot of writing that lacks "story." The characters are passive or uninteresting and I find myself not caring one way or the other whether they survive or die a horrible death. The story is suspended in a timeless place, unanchored and without context, so I don't know where it takes place or why. The character doesn't transform but is exactly the same at the end, and so . . . why did I bother?

A story is not a collection of beautiful descriptions. Or a series of internal ruminations, even if you have 100,000 words. A story is shaped by a series of decisions the author makes around a few key factors:

- a WHO (character or characters);

- a WHAT (theme);

- a WHEN (setting in time and space);

- a WHY (plot); and

- a HOW (structure that supports the story).

Without this invisible architecture holding up the narrative, what you have is some writing, but you do not have a story.

41

Think of your life
as a story

If you've never thought of your life as a story, think about it now. Figure out how your story fits in this glass slipper of a structure. Because getting these elements right is what will make the difference between a boring rendition of all the stuff that happened to you and a story other readers will connect with and care about.

Think of the qualities of all the books and stories in the world that you love. *Romeo and Juliet. Catcher in the Rye. Moby-Dick. Great Expectations. Pride and Prejudice. To Kill a Mockingbird. Beloved. Wuthering Heights.*

What are they about? Forget the facts, give me the guts:

- tragedy
- romance
- comedy
- heroes
- villains
- epic battles of the spirit

Now think of your life. Make columns and list the moments in your life that qualify as:

Tragic	Romantic	Comedic
All you've lost, all you regret	All those you've loved	All those funny stories

Heroic	Villainous	Epic battles
All those times when you rose to the occasion and surprised yourself with strength you never knew you had	All those frenemies, the people who hurt you, tried to screw you over, made you suffer	All those times when you didn't know how you'd make it through, but you did

Once you've figured out what your story is about, you can work out what facts are important to illustrate it for your reader.

42

Survivor

Another way to think about your life is in terms of what you've survived.

Make a list of all the things you've survived.

Accidents

Losses

Failures

Disappointments

Regrets

Having too much of a good time

Losing your way in life

Loving the wrong person

Miscarriages, stillbirths (literal or metaphoric)

Keep going . . .

PART II

Trust

As soon as you trust yourself, you will know how to live.

— Johann Wolfgang von Goethe

43

Say yes

Writing your story begins with you saying YES to yourself.
Yes, writing is worth my time.

Yes, I have something worth saying.

Yes, I will fight for my voice.

Yes, I will work through the doubts.

Yes, I want to understand who I am.

Yes, I trust myself.

Yes, yes, yes.

Writing your story is about developing trust. Trust in yourself, your story, and the process of writing.

44

Only you can believe in you

Even if you do land a publishing deal with a traditional publisher, advance 'n' all, indicating that at least a publisher believes in you, it still doesn't change the fact that only you can believe in you.

I've seen the most talented writers teeter on this precipice. Mentors help. Writing groups hold the space. Getting feedback holds us steady. But ultimately, if you don't finally own in your heart that you can do this, you won't. The conviction might trickle in incrementally, like drops of rain filling a well, with small wins and hard work. It might show up as a sunflower of clarity in your heart that one day just bursts into its bright yellow self. It doesn't matter how it comes, but it must come from deep within you.

Just as some of the most glamorous celebrities who seemingly have it all never feel beautiful, rich, or happy enough, so the external trappings of success as a writer will never turn on that switch of self-belief.

Conviction—trust in yourself—is about grabbing hold of the reins of clarity and riding like hell toward your goal.

45

Stop waiting

We all imagine that now is not the right time. We're busy. We're working. We've got little kids. We're not inspired. But someday, we think, the right circumstances will arrive like a long-awaited parcel in the post. The stars will align. The Age of Aquarius will dawn.

This illusion is catastrophic.

Buddhist teacher Jack Kornfield said, "The problem is, you think you have time." We don't. Now is the right time. It's the only time.

This craziness spills into our expectations once we've finished writing too. We search for an agent. We submit our manuscripts to 1,000 publishers. And we wait. To be picked. To be ordained as worthy. For recognition. For a contract. To be chosen. For our books to become bestsellers.

Here are the hard, cold facts about the publishing industry today: No one is coming to save you (or me, for that matter). No literary agent or publisher is waiting for us to write that bestseller. Even if we get "picked," they are not responsible for our success.

We are.

So stop waiting. A. Lee Martinez wrote, "Those who write are writers. Those who wait are waiters."

Whatever you're waiting for doesn't exist.

Write now.

46

Only connect

Why does our writing fail sometimes?

We fail when we try too hard.

We bomb when we try to copy others.

We miss the mark when our writing is not aligned with who we are.

We write vaguely when we don't really know what we have to say.

We fail when we shrink back from the deepest self-knowledge we are capable of reaching.

The way to connect with our writing voice, ourselves, and our readers is through an intimacy with our felt experience.

To be successful as a writer, we must be good connectors.

We must be connected to our own emotional truths and our authentic writing voice.

47

Stepping into something larger than you

Saying YES doesn't mean that you're not shitting yourself. It doesn't mean you know everything's going to be okay. It's an invitation to the universe to meet you in a bigger vision of who you know you can be.

We trust ourselves when we step into something that is larger than ourselves—when we act even before we're ready, or when we don't quite know what we're doing. It's about taking an action that feels so scary, radical, so much bigger than we think we can fit into, but we believe we'll grow into it, goddamn it. It's Goethe's "boldness"—a cheeky (not delusional, mind you) invocation of a huge energetic container that we must now fill. First we must create our vision, then we must take powerful action to step into that vision. As John Burroughs said, "Leap and the net will appear."

Ten years ago I was in partnership with a wonderful woman. We started a small business writing books for companies. Our time was spent writing proposals and pitching books on relationships for dating sites, and on how to build your own kitchen for hardware stores. I was decomposing inside. These were not the books I was born to write.

But we were making a modest income and we had several projects lined up. All I wanted was to write my new novel. I was terrified to break the partnership, but I did.

"You're crazy," she told me. "We've got a good business here."

I didn't care about the business. I cared about my writing.

"I want to see if I can make it on my own as an author."

She shrugged and gave me that look we give someone when we know they're about to make the biggest mistake of their life.

Her words played into all my deepest fears—of failing, of not making it, of giving up on a sure thing to pursue some ridiculous fantasy of being an author.

I even told her she could keep my share of the business. I wanted a clean start. I needed an uncluttered vision of my future.

The German poet Rilke said, "The future enters us . . . long before it happens."

And I leaped.

48

What do you stand for?

When I was a law lecturer, I once got into a fierce argument with a student while we were discussing rape law. I said it would be a struggle for me to defend a person accused in a rape case (not that sometimes people aren't wrongly accused; it happens—rarely, but it does happen). He reproached me for not being objective. I went away and mulled over our interaction. Was I a flawed legal thinker because of my bias toward rape survivors?

I penned him a long letter in which I wrote that we all have to make choices about who we are and what we stand for in life. We need to draw lines: this is who I am and these are my values. For a lawyer, one of those lines is: *Do I become a prosecutor for the state or do I defend accused people? Do I go into criminal law or corporate law? Do I defend rapists or do I work with rape survivors?*

I explained that of course someone accused of rape deserved the best defense lawyer. But that person wasn't going to be me. Why? Because I wouldn't make myself available in that way. The accused has the right to a lawyer, but he can't have me.

Similarly, I decided early on that I didn't want to be an English professor or a literary critic, because I didn't want to be critiquing work, I wanted to be on the side of creation.

As writers we need this kind of conviction. Not just believing up front in our ability to write, but keeping our belief going. It is no good to be endlessly doubting our story or our ability to tell it. Writers have to be able to make countless decisions—about what to include and not to include, whether and how to write about real people, which word best describes what they're saying, and how to excise whatever is not serving the story. Wishy-washy doesn't cut it. A writer must be able to act with the decisiveness of a surgeon.

In my book *Things without a Name*, I named all the characters after real people who had died in incidents of domestic or sexual violence. At the end of the book there was an appendix in which I told each person's story in a few lines.

My publisher wanted me to drop the appendix. She said it might "make readers uncomfortable," and that "it wasn't appropriate in a work of fiction."

I didn't want to piss my publisher off. But this was so important to me that I refused to budge, and I knew if she refused to publish the book with the appendix, I'd be willing to walk away.

A few years later, when my editor returned the manuscript of my book *When Hungry, Eat*, she recommended cutting out the humor in certain places because she felt it undermined the more serious moments.

"That humor is part of my writing voice," I told her. Still, I went through the manuscript and sweated over each of her suggestions before rejecting most of them. I knew what the feel of the book should be, and humor was at the heart of it. Her vision for the book was simply different from mine. If I hadn't trusted myself, I might have let her talk me out of my own writing voice.

Writers cannot be pushovers. But we must be flexible at the same time. We must pick our battles and work out which ones matter and which ones we're prepared to let go. Above all, we must not be precious about our writing. But we must be able to distinguish between what matters and what doesn't. This takes practice.

49

Take yourself seriously

When you're 18 and you say that you want to be a writer, people respond, "Get a real job." Because you think adults know how life should be lived, you go to law school because that's a good career for a smart woman.

But you stay up all night writing stories. You lie in bed on weekends reading like you're book-malnourished (though law school nearly destroys your love of reading).

You get into an Ivy League university. You go off to do a master's in law, and now you have two law degrees. But one day you wake up in a sweat because if there's one thing you're clear about, it's that you really don't want to be a lawyer.

You make friends with a journalist and confess to her one night after too much red wine that you want to be a writer (*said whisperingly*). She sends you an application form for a writers' colony, a place where you can go and write for weeks on end and be bothered by no one and, in fact, have people cook your meals. That application stays pinned to your bulletin board for a year. Every time you look at it, you brush the thought away and go back to marking first-year law essays on the fundamentals of contract law. Sometimes when you're alone you say out loud, "I want to be an author." Shameful stuff like that. You keep these dirty thoughts to yourself. You keep writing late into the night.

One day after getting into a fight with a law student over the mark you gave him, you pull that form down and fill it in as if you were applying for an organ transplant.

Then you think, *I might as well apply for a few more.*

Even waiting for the rejections feels more hopeful than not having done anything at all. As if you've opened a window you were told never to try to open and now you can finally breathe.

The first rejection letter arrives. You finger the letter and, though it hurts, you know that someone out there actually read your stuff. But then another letter arrives and it's fatter than the first one. *Fat is good,* you think.

And it is. Because you've been offered an eight-week residency at that writers' colony.

Suddenly a wind sweeps in through that open window and you cradle your head and kiss the letter because here it is: the moment that changes everything.

* * *

I was offered places at three of the writers' colonies I applied to. I chose Hedgebrook and spent eight weeks of a Seattle autumn in Cedar cottage, where I wrote the first draft of my debut novel, *The Dreamcloth.*

I don't know how destiny works, but I know I curved the arc of my life that day when my longing to write out-muscled my fear that I couldn't.

When I took that application form down and applied myself to the task of answering hard questions about why I wanted to write and what I wanted to write about, I was saying YES to the part of me that longed to be a writer. We can't ask others to take us seriously until we've taken ourselves seriously. It starts with us.

But taking yourself seriously means taking risks. Getting squirmily uncomfortable. Doing stuff you'd never, ever normally do. Like strip naked in public—at least that's how it feels when you enter short story competitions and send your writing into the world looking for a publisher.

This is where conviction and courage lock arms and we leap to the next level.

There's only one way to test the strength of your conviction that you want to write—and that's by putting yourself out there, getting rejected, regrouping, trying again and again and again and again, until something gives.

Like Olivia, one of the writers I mentor who, in sheer terror, sent off her short story to a competition . . . and won. Her story was then produced and performed on national radio. Then an exquisite piece she wrote for Mother's Day was published and she was asked to read it on national radio. She has now finished the first draft of her book.

And Elana, another writer I mentor, who has just had her 22nd article published—and successfully negotiated a higher per-word rate than she was first offered. Because she now understands the value of her own writing.

And Kerry, who has been on several writing retreats with me, who won a poetry competition and had her second story shortlisted in a regional short story competition.

Treat yourself with dignity and respect. Call yourself a freelance writer. Think and behave like someone who is serious about what she's doing.

50

Trust what you love

Given that we're all born into a language that seeps into us by some magical neurological osmosis, perhaps we're prone, in that peculiarly human way, to take for granted what we already possess. We have words. Having them, we don't think to love them. We're a species notorious for needing tragedy to illuminate our appreciation of what we already have, be it health, companionship, the most ordinary of happinesses. I, for one, am perfectly clear that I do not need to have a stroke wipe out my facility for the English language to be reminded of how much I love words.

In my early teens my father, perhaps finally wearied by my prolific poetic offerings and towers of teetering adjectives, gave me a copy of Dylan Thomas's *Under Milk Wood: A Play for Voices*.

I remember a sensation tingling through my body as I read the opening paragraph:

> To begin at the beginning: It is Spring, moonless night in the small town, starless and bible-black, the cobblestreets silent and the hunched courters'-and-rabbits' wood limping invisible down to the sloeblack, slow, black, crowblack, fishingboat-bobbing sea. The houses are blind as moles (though moles see fine to-night in the snouting velvet dingles) or blind as Captain Cat there in the muffled middle by the pump and the town clock, the shops in mourning, the

Welfare Hall in widows' weeds. And all the people of the lulled and dumbfound town are sleeping now.

The words were chocolates in my mouth. I could taste the phrase "the clip clop of horses on the sunhoneyed cobbles of the humming streets" on my tongue. A champagne of verbal bubbles.

As a child I watched circus trapeze artists with bewildered fascination. I never once thought, *I wish I could do that.* Some people do. They go on to become wonderful circus trapeze artists and to travel the world in caravans, or, in this day and age, probably in airplanes. But when I read Dylan Thomas, I thought to myself, *I wish I could do that.* If you are one of those who make this silent wish, you've got what it takes to become a writer, even if you've never written a single word.

We can use words to say "get lost," "whatever," "all right," "that's nice," but . . . we can also dip into language and use words that uplift and inspire. If you are one of those people who want to create magic with words, you, honey, are a writer.

I studied linguistics in my first year at university, and I vaguely recall decoding sentences to reveal deeply embedded structures, layers upon layers of parts of speech, quite algebraic and formulaic. Until then I never knew how innate composition is to language comprehension, and how invisibly interwoven structure is to meaning. It seemed like inheriting a genetic disposition for, say, classical music or drawing when others need years to learn the art. The talent is bundled into us, complete, awaiting discovery.

Words dance in our brains in a place that connects imagination and language, a secret place we don't even know we're partying in.

How can we not love words?

How then can we not trust what we love?

51

Trust your judgment

We live in a culture that makes us endlessly doubt our ability to make good decisions—about what to eat, who to love, what we think of our bodies, and how to be happy. Parents have so lost touch with their intuition that we read book after book on how to be decent parents, because of course we wouldn't know how to do it by ourselves.

Dr. Benjamin Spock's *Common Sense Book of Baby and Child Care*, first published in 1946, marked a break from the strict routines and discipline advocated by behaviorists who tended to enfeeble parents by labeling them ignorant. The opening lines of his book were simply, "Trust yourself. You know more than you think you do."

I struggle to even follow a recipe because I don't like being told what to do. I trust my instincts, my judgments, and that if I make a mistake, at least I'll learn something about myself.

So I find it bewildering when aspiring writers ask me, "What do you think I should write about?" I don't have the answer to anyone's longing. If we don't trust ourselves, we will never be able to take the risks and make the decisions we need to as authors.

No one else has the right answers to the questions in your heart.

Let yourself be the judge.

Choose.

Then live by your choice.

52

Trust the urgency

I wanted to be a mother from the age of four.

So in my late twenties, when I was a law lecturer, I befriended a guy called Zed who had the office next to mine. After two years, our friendship sidled into the romance zone.

And a month into our relationship I told him, "I want a baby next year. Are you in or are you out?" I come from a line of dodgy uteruses, and my ovaries were all lined up and ready to go.

He choked on his beer and stammered, "I . . . I don't know if I want children."

"I get it," I said. "Kids aren't for everyone. But I'm twenty-eight and I want a baby before I'm thirty."

I gave him a few weeks to think about it.

A year later our daughter was born, and two years after that, our son. We've now been together for 20 years.

When I recount this story—mostly, it seems, while I'm having my hair done by young hairdressers who are being jerked around by commitment-phobic men—they gasp at my audacity. "My boyfriend would run a million miles. How come yours didn't?"

Firstly, Zed is not an asshole.

Secondly, I was unambiguous about what I wanted. I put my needs right out there. Clarity has a magnetic quality, whether we want to be mothers, pole dancers, musicians, or writers. If we're fuzzy, we must work to get unfuzzed. The belief that we have "the rest of our lives in front of us" is a conceit of unmindfulness. It's existentially negligent. We ought to act with some urgency around the things that matter to us.

When we're not clear, we make vague decisions. Vague decisions lead to depression and unhappy life choices that leave us feeling like victims because they seem not to have been made by us as much as they have just *happened* to us. McDonald's is full of such folk. Because if they stopped and asked themselves what they want out of life, they'd know they don't want diabetes, heart disease, and high cholesterol.

We are the only ones who can answer the question *What gives my life meaning?* Not our parents, not our politicians, not our mates, not our girlfriend or boyfriend or spouse. Nothing is more important than knowing what we want in life.

Finally, I wasn't afraid of Zed's answer. If he'd run away, at least I'd have known he wasn't the right guy. The world is full of men to choose from. So if he'd done a runner, I'd have been hurt and sad for a while, but it wouldn't have been the end of my world. What would have been a big deal is if I'd never made my intentions clear, hung around for a few years, and tactfully brought up the kid question only to find out that he didn't want kids just when my ovaries were thinking of going into retirement.

Conviction elicits an equal conviction—meeting ours with either a YES or a NO. When we are clear, and bold, an alchemy is unleashed and we can change our reality.

When we trust ourselves, we know what to do.

53

Trust the innerness

In everything we do—whether it's writing a book, getting married, having children, immigrating, getting divorced, going through a serious health crisis—we can (and should) prepare ourselves as best we can. But there's a part that only happens once we're right in the middle of it all—there's a knowing, a resiliency, a fierce, soulful flame that ignites when we're riding the storm that we can never access in the lead-up because it only kicks in once we're there. And it's THIS deep innerness that we have to learn to trust. The wings we need will grow as we're falling.

Every process has its own mystical quality. We cannot control or predict it. We just need to be aware of it. Writing a book is a process, a slow intimacy that develops over time with language and our voice. Sometimes we get stuck and we don't know how to move a particular scene or moment forward. So we might throw out a question like a bone into the bushes and ask our subconscious mind, like a puppy, to retrieve the answer for us.

After I'd submitted my manuscript for *Love in the Time of Contempt* to my publisher, I was asked to write a final chapter that could somehow "hold" the message of the book. I spent weeks trying desperately to think up a brilliant ending and kept coming up with nothing.

But I've written enough to know to trust the process. It doesn't work to deadline or demand. It's a bit like a teenager in that way.

During this time, I was distracted with a new kitten in our home. We bought Archie from the Cat Protection Society. We'd specifically requested a laid-back kitten to accommodate Tanaka, our queenly dame who'd been around for 15 years and detested other feline company. But as soon as Archie jumped out of his box in our apartment, he dropped the cruiser act and transformed into an alpha-male crazy cat. He tore up and down our hallways, jumped in the trash bins and the fridge, and once even tried to get into the oven. He knocked food off the table, broke dishes, and frankly, he was driving me nuts.

Archie scratched, bit, and drew blood. "He's the worst cat," my teenage son declared. "I hate him."

"He'll grow out of it. And you can't hate him, he's just a kitten," I said.

"What's the point of him? He won't sit in my lap."

"You love him, no matter what he does. You keep hoping he'll come sit with you, and one day when you least expect it, he will. And then all your love will have been worth it, just for that moment."

And suddenly, I knew I'd found the ending to my book on how to love teenagers. I ended it with this paragraph:

> A week after my conversation with my son, I'm walking through the apartment, switching off the lights, and I find him curled up in front of the TV, his long lanky body a gangly sculpture of limbs, his face soft in sleep, his huge feet sticking out from under the zebra-striped TV blanket. I wonder whether I should wake him and send him to bed, but then I notice the white nose and single stretched-out paw peeking out from under the blanket. I turn and let him be.

The right image, the right moment, the right sentence will come to you in time.

Our story is something that happens between our intention and the process of writing. We don't control it entirely. We have to trust that the mulling, the random exploration, the quavering, and the crises will lead us to the end. We have to hold on to the reins of our story and surrender at the same time (yep, that's a paradox).

Trust the innerness.

54

Trust creation

Anne Enright, winner of the Man Booker Prize in 2007, writes in *Making Babies*, "A baby is, first and foremost, an act of the imagination." Procreation is a psychological pirouette into what is possible, a projection into the unknown. We all create from an invisible abundance; though oblivious to it, baby girls are born with hundreds of eggs inside their bodies, as well as the perfect gestation environment for a human life. We may not be aware of it, but that doesn't detract from the fact that it's true. Then, 20 or 30 years later, when we see two little pink lines on a pregnancy test, we have a moment of radical self-disbelief. *Me? Pregnant? How did I do that?*

To write, we have to learn to trust ourselves and what it is we are doing.

This business of creation is grander than us in the most ordinary of ways. Each of us is, unconsciously, involuntarily even, a repository of an infinite potential for creation.

Likewise, we need to trust that all the elements of our story are inside us, even if we can't see them.

One way to do this is to understand why it is that we lack self-belief. The answer's the same for all of us: because we're not sure that our story matters.

55

Trust your story

If you're human and you're breathing, you have a story. From a distance, your life reveals patterns, crises, moments of heroism, and dark nights of the soul. You may have a sense of your storied life already, because it's likely that you've taken to journaling at some point to record those moments:

"That bastard Felix . . ."

"I wish I'd never met her . . ."

"Did I really say that?"

"My boss is a narcissistic sexist . . ."

Journaling is a sign that your story lives. It has a faint heartbeat. But it's a mistake to type up our journals and slap on a book cover.

Trust me when I say that no one should read what we write in our journals. Writing we do late at night or before sparrow call where we splurge on self-indulgence, sloppy emotion, and half-processed thoughts is a private affair. We think it's more fascinating than it is.

But don't diss the drivel. That initial uncensored slobbering onto the page is a dump we have to make before we can sort through the rubble and pick out what we want to share with an audience.

What we write in our journals is not our story. But our story nestles somewhere in there. As we figure out what our story is, we need to remember that not everything we think or write about is interesting to other people. However, once we process the chaos and examine the tangled threads, we will find the captivation our story holds for others. We must not doubt that the ordinariness is fertile and valuable.

Don't lose the strength of your belief that your story matters. It matters to you. Your job is to make it matter to others.

How do you do this?

First, you must think in "story," not in facts.

Second, you must get clear on who you are writing for.

Imagine your book in a reader's hands. Ask, *What's in it for someone who doesn't give a toss about me and my life?* Always write for someone. The energy of that trajectory is grounding and directive.

Trust that your story is the way to your reader as well as the obstacle to your reader. Don't let the facts of your story get in the way of reaching that person's eyeballs and aorta. The facts of your life are only there to illuminate for the reader a truth that transcends them. In later chapters, I will share writing techniques that make space for a reader inside your story.

Hilary Mantel, winner of the Man Booker Prize in 2009 and 2012, said this about memoir:

> It's hard for beginners to accept that unmediated truth often sounds unlikely and unconvincing. If other people are to care about your life, art must intervene. The writer has to negotiate with her memories, and with her reader, and find a way, without interrupting the flow, to caution that this cannot be a true record: this is a version, seen from a single viewpoint. But she has to make it as true as she can. Writing a memoir is a process of facing yourself, so you must do it when you are ready.

We trust our story when we are ready to write or tell it.

So what does it mean to be "ready"?

We are ready when we have some degree of self-awareness (however you choose to get there—meditation, therapy, dance classes, laughter-yoga, tantric visualization, the Hakomi Method . . . you pick). When you've suffered enough and have been broken and rebuilt many times. It's a blend of maturity and empathy and self-compassion and a lot less ego.

Knowing ourselves is critical, but it's not enough. We've got to learn how to transform self-insight into shared insight. We must apprentice ourselves conscientiously to the craft of writing to develop clarity on questions like:

- Why do I want to write this story?

- Who is this story for?

- What is this story about?

- How will I tell this story?

- What is my plan of action?

- What decisions do I need to make?

- What do I still need to learn?

Be humble. And have conviction.

Trusting your story happens when you work the hell out of that impossible contradiction.

56

Trust the universe to follow your clear instructions

M any years ago I was trying to finish the draft of a novel I'd been
working on for years. My concentration and enthusiasm for it
had been interrupted by two pregnancies, births, newborns, toddlers,
and work that was bringing in some much-needed diaper money.

But this time I was Serious. It was Now or Never. I wanted To
Finish. But Finishing is a very different business from Beginning. It
has a particularly exacting energy and requires different emotional
and writing muscles. Whereas beginnings can tolerate the chaos of
inspiration and the various explosions of insight that propel all of us to
write in the first place, finishing is about tidying up afterwards. It's the
clearing away of the dirty plates and the scrubbing down of the floors.
It is the neatening of loose ends and the dusting of surfaces.

The problem is, I am a horrible, simply ghastly housekeeper. I
battle to focus and I lose interest in tidying up when I am halfway
through a drawer or cupboard and surrounded by things I can't work
out whether to store, file, or throw out. Finishing requires us to put on
those rubber boots and wade into the swamp of our creativity armed

with a big black garbage bag. It asks of us ruthless decision making. The cutting away of extraneous bits, the folding down of corners, and the smoothing down of edges. Finishing is the art of narrative origami, with a couple of bloody swipes with a samurai sword.

If Beginning is the interior designer, Finishing is the housekeeper. Beginning is for artists, Finishing is for accountants. To be a successful writer, you have to be able to do both. Writing is a discipline as much as it is a flamboyance.

Though my book had become feral and grown from a few pages on a screen to about seven files, with I-can't-remember-how-many-versions-or-which-one-I-last-worked-on, and three boxes of research, I knew that I had to dive in and work it out. Tax accountants do it all the time; they work their way through papers, one by one, and make some order out of it all.

What I lacked was the confidence that this part (the really hard part) was worth it. That far from it being a futile hobby, like trainspotting or bird-watching, there was a point to it all, an über-rationale. That maybe what I had written was worth the effort and someone might actually want to read it.

Most writers suffer from this crushing lack of self-confidence. Ironically, it often kicks in at a point when we are just about to achieve something, to make a breakthrough, turn a corner, or manifest a transformation. We often don't recognize the guerrilla tactics of our own self-sabotaging psyches.

So in the spirit of mentoring my uncertain self, I made a small card with the words "I AM A WRITER." I laminated it. And on the back of the card, I wrote, "Don't forget the book and the magic it carries. You can do it."

I tacked this card up on my computer screen with adhesive. Each day when I sat down to write, those words looked down on me.

An affirmation is an assertion, a verbal visualization, a pronouncement about a state of affairs. When we assert in the present tense something we wish for in the future, so the theory goes, we create our reality. The power of the declaration makes it so.

I don't know enough about the sacred hidden geometries of intention and how they interact with destiny to say if this really is so. Did that card have any power? I know it got my head right. An affirmation is conviction in motion. It's the way we hold ourselves accountable to the longing inside us.

I no longer cringe when I say, "I am a writer." Though I had been writing for a while, the affirmation made it true in my heart

Give the universe clear instructions. Tell it: I am a writer. Then get back to work.

57

Trust the invisible forces

Whenever I start a book, I set my intention for it. I ask: What do I want to bring into the world with this book? Who do I want it to reach? What outcomes would I love to see happen because of it? What other books is it like? I'm feeling for its shape.

Then I collect all the books that have in some deep way inspired or helped contour the longing that's brought me to write the book and I keep them close by as totems to help me bring my book into the world. I choose some books for their style, their humor, or their feel. I choose others because of the clarity of their message, or the beauty of their prose. I come armed with some intention of what I want to create.

I then do some dreamwriting using the prompt "The book I long to write is . . ." Some preliminary writing (sometimes called "prewriting") to frame our intention sets up an invisible but powerful force field around our work that helps contain it. As writers we must reach for specific goals, whether it's to start a blog, get an article published in a particular publication, or write the first draft of a book manuscript. Our dreams and longings start to gain power as soon as they become clear.

I sometimes think of a book as a dream I am trying to have on the page—it feels that mercurial at times. So I speak to it, I invoke it,

I call to it, I ask it questions. I form a relationship with the invisible forces and trust that they are working together with things visible in a quiet miraculous alchemy to bring about something wholly new.

I also believe in pledging my writing to someone, writing toward a person (dead or alive, real or imaginary). You might dedicate your writing to your late mother, a best friend who lives in another country, the Wizard of Oz, the Dude in *The Big Lebowski*, the spirit of Nelson Mandela, the memory of Daniel Pearl, the heart of Kuan Yin, the teachings of Christ or the Buddha. In the Talmud there's a beautiful saying: "Every blade of grass has an angel that bends over it and whispers, 'Grow, grow.'" Every story needs its angel to guard it and whisper words of precious encouragement. Put a picture of your angel above your desk and let it watch over you as you write.

58

Not so tightly

To get what we want, we need to know what we want. We need to set goals and an intention and move toward them with clarity and purpose, always revisiting the question, "Why am I writing this?"

Our goals give us a direction. Where things get weird is when our intention grows tentacles and becomes attachment. Attachment corrupts conviction. The conviction and commitment we need is to the *process of writing*, not the *outcome*. People come to writing wanting to be published. But that intention might become a stumbling block. Your intention needs to be that you're going to write the best goddamned book / article / short story / poem that you can. Pursuing getting published by Penguin Random House like it's the source of all your life's purpose and future happiness is a recipe for deep unhappiness.

And frankly, it corrupts creation.

Frame your intention. Cast your vision. Invoke the invisible forces.

But don't bet on it. Don't go into debt on it. Don't hold on too tightly.

Just write.

59

Tell no one

When we start writing, we get excited and want to share our happy news like a newly pregnant mother-to-be. We want to blab to everyone, "Hey, I'm writing a book." It's hard to keep a secret as big and beautiful as this.

But we must. If we care about what we're doing, we have to learn to keep secrets.

A writer I mentor sent me a tearful e-mail because her husband (her number one fan and supporter, with whom she was sharing all her writing) had innocently asked her, "So how exactly is this thing going to become a book?"

And just like that, the beautiful clean kitchen of her self-esteem, where she was cooking up her story, got trashed.

Even our biggest fans do not understand never to ask HOW, but WHEN. When is your book coming out? Not how.

Peter Block's wonderful book *The Answer to How Is Yes* helps explain that "how?" is not a creative question, and certainly not an empowering one. It is fear based. And as writers-in-the-making, we do not dabble with that devil.

It is better not to share your writing with the world while it is still a little book-fetus inside you.

If you've ever been pregnant and have seen your little pea with its beating heart on the ultrasound, you don't ask, *How am I going to turn this blob into a baby?* No, you just know that something is growing and that by some magical alchemy of you, God, DNA, folate, and bit of luck, a baby will arrive. When it's ready. You're part of the process, but there are other forces at work too.

It's like that with writing. For a while, it's a little book-blob. It doesn't know yet how it's going to grow its heart and toes and eyelashes. But it will. If we shut up and let it get on with it. Mysteries don't like to be interrogated.

Learning to shut up and keep secrets is essential to the art of gestation. We don't celebrate conception publicly. We wait for birth.

60

Guidelines for trusting yourself

Self-trust is an intimacy we accrue, like all intimacies: with attention and deliberate devotion. There are no rules, no instruction
manual we can follow to achieve it. Here are some practices that have
helped me, which I pass on to you . . .

- Find a steady place inside you that is more solid than
  longing, that is fueled by some ambition and courage. Let
  your writing flow from this place.

- Become as clear as you can about why you want to write.
  Don't stop being curious about the pull writing has for you.

- Encourage yourself the way you'd encourage a child you
  adore who has a dream to do something wonderful. Tell
  yourself, *That's a worthy goal; my story is worth telling.*

- Find a group of other writers who can support and
  encourage you. Hang around with other writers so you can
  be a writer nerd and talk writer stuff.

- Subscribe to writer newsletters and receive writer mail.

- Pretend you're already published. Write the blurb for your
  book and make a mock-up of the cover.

- Write a glowing review of your book-to-be.

- Find a mentor who will help you grow as a writer, one whom you trust to be honest with you.

- Find one book that's been published by the publisher you dream of having publish *your* book. Make sure this book is shit. Real crap. It has to be a book that makes you know with utter certainty that you can write a better one. Keep this book by your desk. Every time you look up from your screen, there it will be—published shit. You will not write shit. If this book could get published, yours will too.

PART III

Triggers

The beginning is always today.

—Mary Shelley

So how and where do we begin?

By now you know you can begin anywhere. This, however, is not much practical help, is it? It's too vague, and we can easily get lost in "anywhere." Too much choice, weirdly, doesn't free us, it censors us. Notice how a deadline or a tight topic concentrates our thoughts and energies? I'd much prefer to be told, "Write about the history of the tampon" than "Write about anything."

So here are some suggestions that can serve as triggers, trails inward to lead you to your story.

61

Little

There was a time when we saw the world uncontaminated, when our naïveté and ignorance allowed us to see everything for the first time. As kids we believed what we were told by the adults we trusted. The movie *Life Is Beautiful* tells the story of Guido, a Jewish-Italian bookstore owner who, together with his young son Giosué, is incarcerated in a German concentration camp during World War II. He turns their existence into a magical game, and in this way, he keeps his child from the horror of their reality. Children trust with blind devotion. Until they don't.

Childhood memories are potent partly because little people are, in the words of Carol Shields in her novel *Unless*, in "a locked closet of unknowing." Children have partial understandings, gaps in their knowledge, and these spaces easily become filled with monsters and Wild Things.

We all arrived clean, uncontaminated. But we may have been exposed early to the toxicity and infectious diseases of life. Many of us had painful childhoods—we lost a sibling or a parent, or faced abuse, illness, bullying, loneliness. As children, that world was all we knew. It was our "normal." So we found ways to survive.

How did you survive your childhood?

Much of our grief as adults has to do with the way in which we have failed the children we were, ignored their dreams, disregarded their needs, forced them to grow up and live out other people's choices and demands. Just about any story from our childhood is interesting if we remember it: the first time we saw snow, how we played tickle-toes with our sister, where we went for comfort, what made us afraid, what made us joyful.

When tackling your life story, write about:

- memories of sounds, smells, tastes from early childhood;

- objects from the past—what you loved or played with;

- your mother and father and other important adults in your life, and the ways in which they were there for you and the ways in which they were not;

- your siblings—the good, the bad, the painful;

- the house you grew up in;

- your pets, favorite toys, hobbies, and how you spent your time as a child when no one was looking;

- who was around for you and who was absent;

- your friends, not only people, but also animals, plants, special secret places, imaginary friends;

- what frightened you;

- what magic you believed in;

- your family's secret and how you found out about it or just intuitively knew it;

- what you thought about adulthood and what you dreamed of becoming when you grew up;

- your most beloved teacher;

- what your mother always told you;

- your grandparents;

- the rules in your home;

- your favorite book;

- your champions—maybe an older brother, a grandmother, an uncle, or a special teacher;

- your bullies—perhaps an older sister, a teacher, a neighbor, or a parent;

- your mother's or grandmother's kitchen;

- your traumas and terrors; or

- the labels used in your family (the black sheep, the difficult middle child, the strange one, the ugly duckling, the princess, the crybaby, the sissy, bossy-boots, the oversensitive one, the lazy one, the irresponsible one).

Trawl through old photographs, if you have them. Begin to write into the prompt "I remember . . ." or "When I was a child . . . ," and see what emerges. One memory will snag another and another, and soon you will find you are remembering moments you thought you'd forgotten. Don't judge them, just record them. Let them come back to you.

Once we open the door and summon these memories in, they acknowledge our invitation. They offer themselves back to us like abandoned orphans. They come home.

62

Naive no more

But there came a time when we woke into an altered consciousness. We started to see the world not through the eyes or beliefs
of the adults around us, but through our own eyes. Our innocence
was either slowly eroded or we were blasted with brutal knowledge—
loved ones die, parents get divorced, fathers are absent, mothers are
depressed, no one lives happily ever after, the world is unfair. We got a
whiff of the gas chamber. We saw a burning monk. There was blood in
our living room. Terrorists struck again. And just like that, the magic
of our childhood was gone.

If childhood was the equivalent of William Blake's *Songs of Innocence*, our teenage years were *Songs of Experience*. Danger, fear, and
shame arrived along with periods, breasts, wet dreams, and pimples.
We began to question and push back against the rules, the injunctions
not to go near the edge, talk to strangers, play with fire, pierce it,
answer back, masturbate, experiment with illegal substances.

Sex arrived. At least the longing for it. And the fantasies coupled
with trepidation.

We rejected, rebelled, sought our own adventures, forged our own paths. We turned our backs on our emotional, social, and philosophical inheritance. We went in search of our own paths.

So you could write about:

- the moment you associate with your "loss of innocence" or when your magic was stolen;

- the betrayals of childhood—who and what let you down;

- loneliness;

- your first kiss;

- your first sexual experience;

- your first decent sexual experience;

- not fitting in;

- the first time you defied your parents or rebelled;

- playing with fire;

- walking away as an act of claiming your selfhood (what were you walking away from, such as parents or expectations, and what self were you claiming?);

- the first time you "experimented" (sexually, with drugs, alcohol, porn, cigarettes, weapons, guns, or anything else you were told to stay away from);

- getting piercings and tattoos;

- mixing with the "wrong crowd";

- risks you took;

- risks you wish you'd taken;

- what it meant to you to "come of age";

- moments of defiance;

- someone who was a great influence on your life, such as a teacher, coach, friend, bully, or mentor (what did they tell you, what did they see in you?);

- how you have rebelled.

If you're reading these prompts and thinking, *I never did that or that or that*, guess what? You missed out. Now write about all the ways in which you got shortchanged on your adolescence and how this plays out in your life today.

63

They may not mean to, but they do

In Philip Larkin's hilarious but sobering poem "This Be the Verse," he reminds us that our parents screw us up, even though they may not mean to. This may come as a relief to those of us who were feeling a little shortchanged in the happy-family department. My sense is that people who come from happy families go on to become preschool teachers and laughter therapists. To be a writer, you probably need a bit of unhappy family history, you know, to work with. As Tolstoy's opening line to *Anna Karenina* reminds us, "Happy families are all alike; every unhappy family is unhappy in its own way."

In the kiln of family, each of us is shaped and dented by how much or how little we were loved in the beginning. We know now that our earliest experiences in our families of origin mold our self-understanding. In our first relationships (with our mothers, fathers, sisters, brothers, grandparents, and extended family), we learned about loss, forgiveness, anger, trust, safety, loneliness, belonging, tolerance, and generosity. Parenting, we're learning, is best undertaken when it's not a part-time hobby and we have our own shit together. But our folks didn't know that.

In those early incubators, we formed our basic understanding of relationships, marriage, and parenthood. We took those blueprints with us into the world and went on to have our own lovers, partners, friendships, and children—or not.

This is fertile ground for exploring our stories.

You can write about:

- three questions you wish you could have asked your father;

- three things you wish you could say or could have said to your mother;

- the first time you fell in love;

- the first time someone fell in love with you;

- yourself through the eyes of your first love;

- someone you feel strongly about (positively or negatively);

- the one person who "gets" you;

- the one who got away;

- unrequited love;

- how you feel about marriage or commitment;

- experiences of infidelity—others' or your own;

- broken families;

- losing someone you loved;

- pregnancy, childbirth, becoming a mother or father;

- all the people you have loved in your life;

- a relationship that ended badly (told first from your point of view and then from the other person's point of view); or

- the three most important relationships in your life and what they have taught you about yourself.

64

Skin and bones

One of the most reliable places to enter your writing is through your body. Why? Because it's there. And as long as you're breathing, it's working.

In *Dubliners*, James Joyce wrote, "Mr. Duffy lived a short distance from his body." We do not want to be like Mr. Duffy.

It doesn't matter how you get into your body as long as you get out of your head. That's where the noise is. You want the silence of sinew, the music of muscle, the beat of blood.

When we don't sink below our chins, our writing can become abstract and incorporeal: "The oceans float . . . clouds of life . . . strips of light . . . harmony . . . heaven swivels . . ."

It's heady, a bit "'what does this even mean?" And the minute a reader has to stop and ask *What does this mean?* we've lost them. So one way to make sure we stay focused is to tether ourselves to skin and bone. We want to make sure that when we write about oceans, we're talking about colors (the white lace hem of the water) and sounds (the shushing of waves on sand). That we're tasting, smelling, feeling. From these embodied descriptions, we can take the reader on a journey into the emotion that the "bitter brine" or "silver stretch of water like satin" evokes.

As writers, we want to live right in the heart of our bodies. We want to be able to share and communicate the full sensual experience of what it is like to feel hungry, afraid, lost, in pain, in love—the whole glorious catastrophe of what it means to be human.

Our writing voice is the guts of our writing. To find it, we have to go deep down into our belly. So get inside your skin. Write about physical experiences and sensations.

We have five windows into our bodies—the senses. Choose any of them. Though we all see, hear, touch, smell, and taste, each of us does it differently, in ways that are unique to us. Some of us see colors; others see shapes. Some of us notice the spaces around things more than the things themselves. Some of us hear too much, some of us hear undertones, and some can only hear the silences.

When we see things, we tend to hardly look at them. We gloss over. We glance. We don't allow ourselves to pause in the sensual experience. Remember in the movie *The Lion King* when Rafiki leads Simba to water and Simba says, "That's not my father. That's just my reflection"?

Rafiki says, "Look harder."

Find ways of seeing you have not seen before. Look for what you cannot see. Gustave Flaubert wrote, "Anything becomes interesting if you look at it long enough."

One way to make sure we are looking harder is to come to things curiously, never assuming we know what is there. It's this kind of sensory curiosity that helps us avoid lapsing into mundane thinking and cliché. When we look at clouds, faces, oceans, we want to see the way *we* see, not recycle Wordsworth or Eliot or something we saw on Facebook.

Write about:

- what you see when you look in the mirror and how you acquired the lines on your face or a particular feature;

- what emotions arise when you look at your face;

- the stories your skin tells—scars, freckles, wrinkles;

- music that moves you—how it feels in your body;

- the silences—let quietness talk to you;

- the tastes of different foods in terms of color and memory—
  dark chocolate, licorice, a clove, cumin seeds, an olive,
  fresh mint;

- a time when your body surprised you;

- a time when your body let you down;

- the worst pain you've ever felt;

- the most intense physical pleasure you've ever experienced;

- what your vagina or penis would say, in two words, if it
  could talk;

- your toes, eyelashes, cheeks, chin, thighs, breasts, hands,
  lips, knees, ears, bellybutton, thumbs, neck, hips, forehead,
  shoulders, bottom, feet, eyes, arms, back, tongue, nose;

- a body part you feel ambivalent about—write a dialogue
  between you and this body part in which it makes a case for
  why you should like it more;

- whether your body is a friend or an enemy;

- whether your body is treacherous or trustworthy;

- a secret your body keeps;

- the worst sex you ever had;

- the most delicious thing you ever tasted; or

- when you first noticed your gender and how you
  feel about it.

65

Where it aches

The great cellist Gaspar Cassadó used to say to his students, "I'm so sorry for you, your lives have been so easy. You can't play great music unless your heart's been broken." I believe this is true of writing too. I'm not one to romanticize hardship or grief, but we all know that we have to have a truthful conversation with these ouchy places. They do not sink quietly away. They have an energy and life force and if we tap into them, they become a source of our own creativity. Happiness is often more difficult to write about. It can be boring, unless it is fragile or hard-won. As the wonderful Buddhist teacher Pema Chödrön said, "If it's painful, you become willing not just to endure it but also to let it awaken your heart and soften you. You learn to embrace it." For each of us, there is a place where our suffering started. That's where the pain of our past sits, waiting for us to find it.

I don't believe we always have to write *about* our pain, but we do have to write *from* it. Because emotion is the key to connection with a reader—it's one of the elements of what I call "transition," where we cross the bridge from the personal to the universal. Our reader may not have been bullied, lost a limb, buried a child, or gone through our personal hell, but every single person knows love, loss, grief, pain, regret, guilt, and sorrow.

Explore how *you* experience grief, love, shame, desire, hope, fear, joy, loneliness, passion, pain, elation, regret. Get down deep into those gritty emotions. Imagine them as characters in your life. What is your relationship with them? No one feels them in the exact way you do. Because here's the kicker: you can only take a reader as far as you have gone. So, how far have you really gone? Can you go further?

In later sections on Techniques, I'll talk about "touch and being touched" and "telling the truth"—both essential components for finding your unique writing voice.

For now, it's enough to know that you can begin your story by writing about:

- things that make you happy (in an interesting way, because happiness is not that interesting all by itself);

- what has brought you to your knees;

- your deepest regrets;

- the saddest you have ever been;

- the worst stress you have ever experienced;

- the deepest peace you have ever known;

- a time when you couldn't find a way to go on;

- an emotion that dominates your life (fear, anxiety, loneliness, anger, hatred, joy, regret);

- a time when you panicked;

- a time when you were truly conflicted and how you resolved it;

- a time in your life when things did not work out and fell apart around you;

- jealousy;

- anxiety;

- any other emotion.

66

Shhh

The most interesting characters in fiction have secrets. A concealed vice. A hidden identity. An undisclosed addiction. A past trauma (or "backstory wound," something from the past that will disrupt their desire or goal in the front story). Secrets emit energy, like static electricity, and run like an undercurrent through the narrative. They keep our reader twitching, turning the page, wondering, *What's really going on here?* Until the moment of revelation, we haven't really known the character at all. (This is good to remember in real life when we judge people based on a single impression without having walked a day in their moccasins.)

Fictional characters are no different from real people. We all have secrets. We've all sinned. Failed, both spectacularly and privately. We each have our trove of *I wish I'd never*s and *I'd rather forget*s bottled up, buried, disowned, and stuffed in our internal closets. We all pray no one ever finds out about them. These are the orphans of consciousness, the unloved, unwanted bits of us we hope will disappear and never return to claim us as their rightful owners.

But in the poet Rilke's words, "Where I am folded in upon myself, there I am a lie." In this way, secrets turn us all into liars and pretenders. When we don't embrace the fullness of our being—the broken as well as the brave, the fool as well as the philosopher, the loser as well as the lucky—not only are we living in half of ourselves, we're inhabiting the most boring part of our identity.

Think about it. Invariably it's someone's most disgusting habit, deepest regret, most neurotic phobia, or cruelest remark that makes them fascinating. Stories are not made more interesting by emotionally and financially stable heroes. Those who've emerged from perfect childhoods and stride confidently into ideal adulthoods. Well-rounded, hang-up-free folk are not even vaguely intriguing. Soul-stirring stories swarm around the tormented, tortured, and damaged among us. We may not choose to co-parent with such individuals, but we can't deny they make us giddy with adrenaline.

When we write our story, the biggest mistake we can make is to think we must present a flawless front. No one cares about our perfection, so we can drop that facade. Instead, we can become more human to our reader by exploring our hidden territories. Yep, those scary places we were hoping were long forgotten.

So where should we look? We all have our own version of a devastating shame, life-changing regret, or crippling guilt—for an infidelity, abortion, illicit liaison, act of violence, sexual encounter, hurtful thing we said or loving word we didn't offer, trick we played that went wrong, recreational drug or Botox habit we can't shake, love we lost, or child we gave up for adoption.

Secrets wield power, and the deeper we hide them, the more power we give them. In October 2004 "accidental artist" Frank Warren invited people to post him their secrets on homemade postcards when he began a community art project in the United States. He was overwhelmed by the response as hundreds of thousands of people all over the world sent in their secrets. Thus began PostSecret, which has become an international phenomenon, including a series of books and a blog. Here is a selection:

Sometimes I think that if I just got really sick, I'd find out who my true friends are.

My dog winks at me sometimes. I always wink back in case it's some sort of code.

I have been in love with you since you bought those shoes in Zagreb—1,269 days ago.

I am a regular guy who's hiding huge tits under his clothes.

When we're on a business trip together, I secretly hope a random stranger will remark what a great couple we are and that will make you see we should be a couple.

Being anonymous, you might think, would take the fun out of the secrets, but strangely, not. Secrets are addictive because they reveal dimensions of human frailty. As we identify with the shame, regret, anxiety, sadness, or joy in them, we start to feel a space open inside us where we feel safe to be vulnerable. It's the parts we've kept hidden that unite us as human beings and make us feel less alone with our secrets. PostSecret has created an anonymous community of acceptance, which has in turn helped many people accept themselves.

We can repress our secrets, or share them privately with friends, lovers, a group of other addicts, or anonymously on PostSecret, or slowly pry them off our souls like barnacles during years of therapy. Our secrets can become catalysts for life crises and personal growth. We can even recycle them into novels.

But airing our secrets is a prerequisite for healing. We cannot heal what we do not acknowledge. A secret can become a prison for the soul, a way of staying hidden from others and ourselves in what author and medical intuitive Caroline Myss has termed "woundology," where we allow our wounds to control us. Confession in various religious forms acknowledges that the truth sets us free. As Frank Warren, the founder of PostSecret, is fond of saying, "Sometimes when we think we are keeping a secret, that secret is actually keeping us."

Finally, secrets are wonderful intimacy currency. Trust in relationships accrues when our secrets are held with tenderness by others.

When we are loved in all our naked imperfection, we learn that we are worth loving and we make it safe for others to share their secrets with us. As the poet Adrienne Rich says, when we tell the truth, we create the possibility for more truth around us.

But of course that depends on just how deeply we crave the truth. Sometimes we prefer the power of our secrets more than we desire the liberation of the truth.

With this in mind, you can write about:

- the ways in which you know you are pretending or posturing;

- the one thing you're most afraid someone will find out about you;

- your secret selves (the parts of yourself that others don't know);

- an incident in your past that still haunts you;

- a habit or addiction you've unsuccessfully tried to give up;

- something you deeply regret;

- your deepest fears;

- the truth you are blurring;

- what you are afraid to simply say;

- what you're unwilling to face;

- a time when you were obsessed with something or someone;

- a time when you were out of control;

- an unrequited love;

- the worst lie you've ever told;

- the worst lie you've ever told yourself;

- your hidden talents, your untapped potential (who or what you would have liked to be);

- a dream or goal that you didn't achieve (what went wrong and how your failure changed you);

- madness (either in yourself or in the world);

- an incident that could be used against you if you ever ran for political office;

- 10 minutes that still make you cringe; or

- your worst vanity.

67

Entering the forest

O nce we're comfortable with the idea that we all have secrets (stowaways in our psyche we're knowingly concealing)—we're not far off from wondering what else might be lurking in the forests of our consciousness, that complex, layered internal space we often only touch on in therapy or deep meditation.

These are the parts of us that are in shadow. The shadow is known by many names: the dark side, the lower self, the other, the double, the dark twin, the disowned or repressed self, the id, meeting our demons, wrestling with the devil, the dark night of the soul, a descent to the underworld, or a midlife crisis.

I once wrote a poem called "Do not do no harm," which begins:

Do not be

harmless

as the Buddhists teach.

There is no grit in goodness.

No pearl without sand.

No butterfly whose wings

have not been distressed.

Poet Robert Bly called the shadow "the long bag we drag behind us." As we grow, whatever doesn't fit our idealized sense of self or who we want to be becomes our shadow. It's the unknown, dark side of our personality, often inhabited by primitive, socially unacceptable emotions and impulses such as lust, greed, rage, envy, selfishness. We're taught that these are wrong, deplorable, and evil. As socialized, civilized human beings, we distance ourselves from them. We remove them from the deck. We play with a smaller hand. We flatten. We tuck the untidy bits away.

You must break promises

to yourself and others;

do the unforgiveable;

torture those you love;

hunt the fox

and then eat

its fear-stained flesh.

Jung reminded us that we can never elude the shadow. It is a "primordial part of our human inheritance." Whenever these emotions surge through us, these gross, ghastly gremlins, we feel guilty and ashamed. We renew our efforts to suffocate them with more murderous intent.

So how does the shadow manifest if it's so well hidden? A sure sign that the shadow is at work is when we project a trait onto others to avoid confronting it in ourselves.

"She's so needy."

"He's such a loser."

"Homosexuals are perverts."

"I don't like fat/Asian/Muslim/disabled people."

Whenever we dislike a trait in someone else or are repelled by certain kinds of people, our shadow beckons. If our idealized self is obedient and responsible, we may find that we sometimes act out of character (a cue to investigate). Other clues are feelings of contempt, disgust, or reprehension towards others. As soon as we dehumanize or demonize other races, genders, religions, or people who are unlike us, we're working in our own shade. This is how our shadow leaves a trail of bread crumbs. And if we are brave enough and willing to enter the forest, we may learn something about ourselves that will help solve the puzzle of our identities. Of course, this can be scary.

Robert Bly writes, "We spend our life until we're 20 deciding what parts of ourselves to put into the bag, and we spend the rest of our lives trying to get them out again."

Writing is the act of leading ourselves into this forest. When we write, we touch and are touched by our shadows. All of us have edges, taboos, places that scare us. We cannot tell the truth or write from a place of self-knowledge without embracing this murky terrain and bringing responsible awareness to aspects of ourselves that we have kept in the dark.

Jung wrote, "One does not become enlightened by imagining figures of light, but by making the darkness conscious." He paid special attention to the work of integrating the shadow and claimed it was an initiation to an awakened life, an essential awareness for our self-realization. Our job as writers is to bring a lantern into these unlit territories.

Writing is a way of healing the split between our conscious sense of self and who we might be. When we integrate the shadow, we create a unifying awareness, we balance the paradox, allow for ambiguity, and avoid being a cliché.

All this you must do

to learn that there is nowhere to go

no one to become unless you

turn your face

towards the threat inside you.

Not until you learn

where you are jagged

brutal

irredeemable

will you become

visible to yourself.

But remember—it's our shadows that make each of us fascinating. Readers do not want to hear about our good behavior, our perfect marriages, our happy families. Yawn. Always remember: you are a character in a book and characters are only as captivating as their most disgusting habit, most shameful secret, or deepest fear. Your job is to be interesting.

Wherever we sense a warning—"Beware of the edge"—that's where our shadow lives. Each of us has our own edge. Only we know where that edge is.

To find your edge, you may want to look at your internal taboos and delve into unexplained feelings such as:

"I hate my father."

"'I can't remember anything about my childhood."

"Gay people disgust me."

"I hate my own child."

"I get jealous when my husband shows affection to my daughter."

"I find pornography degrading, but I'm also turned on by it."

"I'm attracted to men who are abusive."

Essential to this exploration is that we must suspend judgment of ourselves. We're simply exploring an aspect of who we are out of curiosity in the service of understanding ourselves more fully.

Like the earth is torn

you are torn.

Like it is broken

so are you.

To do no harm

is to

shrink from shadow

as if it weren't

in you,

from you,

like the outbreath

In writing your story, find your shadows. Write about what you don't want to understand and what you're afraid of understanding. Explore forbidden thoughts such as:

- feeling you may have married the wrong person;

- wanting to run away;

- desiring sex with someone of the same sex as you if you identify as heterosexual or with someone of the opposite sex if your primary preference is same-sex;

- wondering what it would feel like to kill someone;

- wanting to have sex with someone half (or double) your age;

- feeling your children would be better off without you;

- fantasizing about killing yourself;

- wanting to have sex with your best-friend's spouse or partner;

- having a favorite child; or

- wondering whether you're capable of murder.

Ask yourself the question you don't want to know the answer to. Write about the thing you think you CANNOT write. Enter that forest with curiosity and see if you too can develop a liking for shadows. They are rich territory for our writing.

68

Tribe

There are a thousand trails inward. Any number of paths that lead to the overwhelming questions every human life must answer: *Who am I? Where did I come from? And why am I here?*

Another trigger for self-inquiry is the investigation of the kinship networks, extended families, histories, religions, ethnic groups, and cultures that have shaped us. As our individual identities begin to emerge, we often bash up against the norms and expectations of these powerful institutions that bear down on us like existential gravity. This sets up a fascinating and fruitful tension for us to explore our emerging consciousness. *Who am I in relation to the group? Where does the family end and I begin? Who am I allowed to become? What am I allowed to believe?*

In this way we begin to understand ambiguity. And if there is anything interesting about each of us, it resides in the mercurial, ever-changing space of paradox.

History is our backstory. All of us are entangled in the collective stories of culture, family, and tradition that precede us. Our job is to disentangle ourselves and retell the story of who we are in relation to the past. Old photographs, documents, stories, and objects might pique our curiosity and trigger an exploration.

A writer I mentor became interested in writing her family's story because of an engraved silver tea service she inherited. She began to investigate its significance and so found a way into her memoir.

In writing *When Hungry, Eat,* I began to wonder why my grandfather came to South Africa from Eastern Europe. I discovered ancestors on my mother's side who originally came from Australia (and emigrated to South Africa) and are buried in Melbourne. Eight years later, I received an e-mail from a distant relative in Canada who, while doing a random Google search, chanced upon my book, in which I name them. Through writing my memoir, I discovered family that had been lost through emigration.

If a tribal, religious, national, or cultural identity feels strong to you—either positively or negatively—it's worth investigating and looking for gaps, stories, missing links, and patterns that have made you who you are. How have these group identities impacted you, and how do they continue to influence who you are?

You can write about:

- the stories that make up your religious, ethnic, family, or tribal histories;

- what you need to make visible in your own history;

- what you need to remember and what you need to forget;

- how your gender, race, age, sexual orientation, or religion defines your identity;

- how women are (or were) treated in your family, religion, or tribe;

- how intermarriage or homosexuality are regarded in these groups;

- traditional or religious messages that were handed down to you;

- guilt that was passed on;

- who wielded power in your family;

- who the scapegoat is or was;

- who acted or acts as the silent heart;

- who is or was criticized in your family;

- what was honored in your family;

- proverbial wisdoms handed down in your family, culture, or tribe;

- what experiences of your family or culture these proverbs reveal;

- the rituals that connect you to your family, religion, group, or tribe;

- the festivals you celebrate as part of your identity;

- the food associated with these rituals, including its preparation and how it is eaten;

- any initiation rituals you have undergone;

- any rites of passage that are considered important, and why;

- the three most defining aspects of your identity and why you chose these three;

- the historical messages you inherited about your identity;

- loyalty and secrecy (part of the unspoken "tribal" messages we receive is that we stick together, we don't talk about what happens in our group to outsiders, we stand by each other) and the secrets you wish you could spill about your family or group; or

- the greater truth you believe would emerge if these secrets were debunked.

69

What I believe . . .

L et's go back to why we're writing our story.

At its core, it's because we want to share what we believe about life, whether it's that *we are here to make a difference*; *love is the only wealth worth accumulating*; *forgiveness is the only way to heal*; or *our suffering either has (or does not have) a larger purpose.*

So what do you believe? What are the overarching values, ethics, and principles of your life?

All story is, in some way, a homage to these beliefs. If we don't have a firm grip on our values, we're going to battle with understanding why we're writing and why anyone would want to read our story. So our task, as we write, is to get clarity on these core principles. What we stand for. What our life is in service to. We need to come armed with clarity about our own emotional truths and the ways in which we are courageous and creative. Whether we're conscious of it or not, our story is a tale about faith, inspiration, and devotion (or its alternatives), and writing it is about honoring the work of our lives.

Once we're clear, we don't want to bash the reader over the head by didactically declaring our philosophies on life, sex, and death. Why not? Because nobody needs a lecture. Rather, we implicitly express these deep beliefs by the way in which we frame and share our experiences.

How we write about our lives reveals whether we believe life is random or karmic. Benevolent or malicious. A gift or a curse.

What happens if we don't know what we think or believe about anything?

Ah, just start writing. Freewriting. As we write, we begin to sense the shape and form of our deepest values, though they might feel inaccessible to our conscious minds.

Another way we can access the invisible, mysterious aspects of ourselves is through dreams. Hélène Cixous writes, "Dreams remind us that there is a treasure locked away somewhere and writing is the means to try and approach the treasure. And as we know, the treasure is in the searching, not the finding. . . . To reach [this risky country where the treasure resides] you have to go through the back door of thought."

Another gateway into this realm is through our relationship with the elements—earth, wind, water, and fire. As we begin to explore our stories, we can engage with the earthiness of being grounded, the flightiness of wind, the fluidity of emotion, and the passion of fire. A connection with nature (the environment, the animals) brings up issues of trust, respect, responsibility, and personal honor.

You can write about:

- a moment of awakening (the birth of a child or some other spiritual experience);

- what you believe in (God, nature, Spirit, Gaia, or nothing at all—what beliefs and values inform your life, and how you hold what is mysterious and unknowable);

- what matters to you;

- what you would die for;

- what you'd be willing to sacrifice to protect your deepest truth;

- the time when you felt closest to God, nature, or Spirit;

- an important dream that meant something to you;

- a time when you acted on instinct;

- a time when there was a strange synchronicity of events or coincidence that changed your life;

- your relationship with silence;

- a time of crisis when you turned to the invisible forces for help;

- your relationship with prayer;

- why you think some people suffer more than others;

- a time when you'd lost all hope and how you recovered;

- what holds you up when life seems most discouraging and hopeless;

- 10 things that give your life meaning;

- experiences that have affirmed your sense of why you're here on this earth;

- experiences that have shaken or disturbed your sense of meaning;

- your relationship to miracles, such as the most miraculous event or experience you've witnessed or encountered;

- what you are no longer certain of;

- what remains unresolved in your life;

- what you must bury;

- what you know you must let go of;

- where the flow in your life is;

- where the source of personal illumination and heat is; or
- where the yin and yang energies (male and female) reside in you.

PART IV

Techniques

Art is fire plus algebra.

— Jorge Luis Borges

Now that we've covered some of the topics you could use as triggers for writing your story (your "what"), we need some technique. This is the "how" part of the book. It's the algebra to your fire. Technique isn't sexy, but it makes your writing sexy.

Never skimp on form. It's lazy. It's disrespectful to your reader. And it's an injustice to your story.

In the chapters that follow, I will share with you what I consider to be the essential techniques you need to write your story so others will want to read it.

And just a reminder for the how-to-write-a-book junkies: I've created my own names for some traditional writing concepts to rearrange and air out well-worn ideas. When a concept becomes a cliché, we may forget that perhaps we didn't fully understand it to begin with. This doesn't mean we're stupid. It's up to our teachers to unpack material in all kinds of new ways until we get it. So that's what I've done.

I find the best way to dive into technique is to read a chapter, and then experiment. Don't let the technique overwhelm you. Allow it to do its job, which is simply to offer structure and make sense of the deep, encoded mysteries of story. It's to make the implicit explicit.

It's to tame and give shape to your fire.

70

Target (or, one size never fits all)

Whenever I give a talk, I ask the organizers for a detailed breakdown of who's in the audience. I want to know if it's women only, or men too. Young or old or a mix? I want prior notice of dignitaries, rabbis, imams, young mothers, teenagers, and children. This is mainly so I don't say "fuck" and offend anyone by talking about menstruation or vibrators. But also, knowing who I'm speaking to changes how I deliver my message. I tailor what I say and how I say things so that what I say has the best chance of landing with my listeners.

The same goes for writing our story.

Who are we writing for?

Earlier I said that you are writing for you. That doesn't change. You must always be writing for you first.

But you are also writing for someone else. Aim your writing at your reader.

So who is your reader?

The answer is never "everyone."

Ever been to a store and tried on a garment with the audacious label "One size fits all"? I am not far off six foot and have thunder thighs. My sister-in-law is five foot two and has a tiny waist. There is no garment on the planet that we could both fit into. I now boycott anything that says "One size fits all," because:

a.   it's clearly a lie;

b.   the manufacturer obviously thinks I'm stupid;

c.   it generally means something I am not—little and skinny.

So who are you writing for? The who always flows from the why—why are you writing your story? Is it to record your history? Then perhaps it's for your family, your children and grandchildren. If you are writing your story to inspire other people and you believe your story could benefit a wider audience, identify who that audience might be, whether it's young mothers, other sufferers of depression, or other cancer survivors. Try not to, in Kurt Vonnegut's words, "open a window and make love to the world." This, he claimed, will only give your story pneumonia.

Do not write until you know who you're writing for and why they would be interested in your book. That's like sewing a dress before you've taken the measurements of the person who's going to wear it. Your book has a target. Let's call her Mary, because that makes her real. How old is Mary? Where does she live? Is she single, married, gay, straight, childless, or maternally overburdened? Where does Mary like to shop? What sort of problems does Mary have? What does she worry about? What TV shows are her favorites? What keeps Mary up at night? Is she menopausal? Who does she vote for?

Always speak to the person in front of you. Always speak to your Mary.

Because Mary is not a fool. She (like you and me) knows one size never fits all.

71

Time line—things that transpired (TTT)

Sometimes the easiest way to dive into our story is by making a time line of important moments and events in the order in which they happened. The benefit of this is that it can serve as an outline of our story. Outlining is a prewriting process where we categorize and organize our ideas before we begin to flesh them out.

Use a table like this:

Date	Age	World events	Big moment in my life	Comments: memories, associations
August 1967	5	Six-Day War in Israel Communist China announces explosion of its first hydrogen bomb	Dad dies	Cemetery, all those flowers in the house, Mum allergic She gets Grandma to throw them in the garbage

Date	Age	World events	Big moment in my life	Comments: memories, associations
January 1968	6	Martin Luther King, Jr., assassinated *Apollo 8* orbits the moon and takes first images of Earth from space	We move to the country	We finally get a dog I have to share a room with Sally Mum starts work as a nurse She's never home
January 1974	12	Richard Nixon resigns Movies: *Chinatown, The Godfather: Part II, Day for Night, Blazing Saddles, The Towering Inferno*	Get my period	Playing tennis, the stain on my tennis skirt Katie gives me her sweater to wrap around my waist
April 1975	13	Pol Pot and Khmer Rouge take over Cambodia. Saigon is surrendered. End of Vietnam War (April 30)	Mum remarries	Hate the wedding, Joe tries to make me dance with him. I cry in the closet

In addition to the personal, include what was happening in the world around you at the big moments in your life. Look at world events as well as local events. You may notice interesting things. For example, if your mother suffered a heart attack in 1945, which was when World War II ended, speculate about the impact of these big themes on smaller events in your life. The world is a canvas and we can interpret how the bigger picture bled into our personal lives. These connections offer poetic backdrops for us to draw on. Look at the movies and books and pop culture that dominated each year. They may trigger new memories for you. Infoplease.com is a great site to help you gather this information quickly.

By creating a time line, we satisfy a few elements of storytelling:

- our time line situates our story in a time and place, so we have a *setting*. Setting is the historical, political, or physical landscape of our book. It helps the reader have a sense of place, both in time and in the space of where our story is set. A historical framework will enrich our story and give it a flavor. We can describe the weather, the architecture, the mood, the streets, what was on TV, the sounds and smells of the time. Sometimes the setting can absorb some of our theme. If our theme is loneliness, we may find elements of our setting that illuminate a sense of isolation (a single potted plant, a house at the end of a street where no one ever passed by).

- we create the basic elements of *plot* (which I will cover in more depth later). The plot of our story is: A led to B, which in turn led to C.

We are not bound to follow the sequence of our time line—it simply lays the tracks for our story. It does not dictate the way we choose to tell it. We will no doubt find a far more interesting way of structuring revelation. We'll move around our time line when we come to curating it for a reader. That's where the craft of storytelling comes in—when we decide how to structure or tell our story.

In memoir, it may seem as if we don't have a lot of work to do to construct our plot. It's already somewhat formed because our life happened as it happened. But remember, a plot is not just A happened, then B happened. It's B happened because of A. In *Aspects of the Novel*, E. M. Forster writes,

> A plot is . . . a narrative of events, the emphasis falling on causality. "The king died and then the queen died" is a story. "The king died, and then the queen died of grief" is a plot. . . . Consider the death of the queen. If it is in a story we say "and then . . . ?" If it is in a plot we ask, "why?"

Our job is to find what is interesting about the Things That Transpired and make causal connections between events we may not, until now, have realized were related.

We're looking for the "whys" as well as the "whats."

Just remember: your story needs a plot to really live and work for the reader.

72

The teller of the tale

Just like in every story, ours must have a fascinating character. In memoir, tag, we're it. Instead of making characters up as we do in fiction, we have to nail ourselves down in memoir. There are unique challenges when we write our own story because we're juggling three roles:

- the narrator or the teller of the tale;

- the protagonist or main character; and

- the interpreter who is trying to make sense of the story.

Still, all the rules of writing character apply. So we must come across as:

- complex and interesting, so our "Mary" will want to know more about us; and

- flawed and sympathetic, so our "Mary" will care about us when, frankly, she has laundry to attend to, not to mention *Game of Thrones* to watch.

But how do we pull off writing about ourselves as a compelling character? We know ourselves so intimately, how do we look back at ourselves and articulate what a reader needs to know about us?

Some suggestions:

- **_Take yourself on a blind date:_** What questions would you ask yourself if you were a stranger to yourself? What have you done that's remarkable or unusual? What are your passions? Weird habits? Be curious about who you are so you can discern your motives, idiosyncrasies, and personality tics. When you write about yourself, you must bring this writer's eye to your own life.

  I recently worked with a writer who couldn't articulate why he might be interesting to a reader. On examination, I pointed out that he had a history of impulsive, rash behavior that invariably resulted in him making exactly the right choices—they'd led him to become so successful that he was able to retire at the age of 43. Where he saw "That's just me," I saw powerful intuition and remarkable courage to act on it.

  Likewise, another writer I mentored failed to mention to me that she was the first female Pipe Major of Hamilton Caledonian in New Zealand. She had a long history of playing the bagpipes, but didn't think this was "interesting enough" to share. When we began to unpack why she began to play and what the pipes represented, she realized this was core to her story.

  Familiarity, in this situation, breeds blindness. We are inured to our own intriguing qualities.

- **_Be objective:_** When we write about ourselves, we must observe our lives as if we were not in them. What do others see when they look at us? When we write about ourselves, we're both inside and outside our story at the same time, a witness as well as captive to the moments we are writing about. Step outside yourself. Look in.

- *Forget what you know:* We can't help knowing how things turned out in our lives since we lived through them—we know that he eventually proposed, and that we accepted. We know that our mother died a year after her cancer diagnosis and that our first pregnancy ended in a miscarriage. When writers write fiction, they must create suspense, tension, and unknowability: Did she buy that one-way ticket? Did he die in the boating accident? Was she unfaithful? It's this suspense that we need to mimic in writing memoir. So we must try to forget what we know. We must unknow "how things turned out" and write as if we too are wondering what happened next.

- *Interview yourself:* In fiction, we may do character interviews to get to know our characters. Likewise, in memoir we can interview ourselves as if we were a character in a book.

  How do we act as both interviewer and interviewee?

  When I was little, I used to play teacher-teacher. I used to set tests for my students, but as I had no students, I had to fill in all the answers and be all the students as well as the teacher. Step in and step out. Same here.

- *Write about yourself in the third person:* By simply changing the pronoun from "me" to "he" or "she," we can sometimes access this "characterization of the self," because the third-person voice can break the thread of over-identification with the narrator: "She who loves to dance in the rain." "She who is a rancid bitch until she's had her first sip of coffee in the morning." "She who won't take out the rubbish on a Tuesday because, goddamnit, it's *his* job."

- **Identify your desire:** A character becomes compelling because of what she or he wants, even, as Vonnegut said, "if it's just a glass of water." So we must identify what we want, whether it's a postage stamp, a date with the hot guy, or to exact revenge against our stepfather. It's this desire pushed up against a series of shitty obstacles we face that creates conflict. So perhaps we start off wanting acceptance, safety, to get over our grief, to forgive our parents, to make peace with our body or our history, to forgive ourselves, to understand why things happened the way they did.

  But often there lurks a deeper desire that is only revealed as the story unfolds. In *When Hungry, Eat*, I start off wanting to lose weight. As the plot progresses, it becomes clear that what I really want is to fit in, to belong, to find a home in my new country. Play around with explicit desire and see if there's a shadow longing hiding underneath.

  The narrative moves forward (and readers keep turning pages) because of *thwarted* desire. So we must identify what we want (or think we want) and then thwart the shit out of that desire.

- **What's at stake?** What happens if we don't get what we want? How compelling is our desire? The author Stanley Elkin said, "I would never write about someone who was not at the end of his rope." The more captivating our reason for wanting something, the more readers will be engaged by our story. So we must figure out what we want; why we want it; how badly we want it; what we're prepared to do to get it, and what we're willing to risk.

- **Point of view:** In memoir, we're telling our story from our point of view. Readers know what we are thinking and feeling.

  But there may be times when we need to shift into someone else's point of view, for example, when we want to convey facts we couldn't have known or when the story is about different perspectives. I'm going to briefly cover the options here.

First person: E.g., "'I was born into a family of neurotics and hypochondriacs."

- **When to use a first-person narrator:** When the story is mainly about the narrator's emotional journey. The reader knows it's all told from that person's perspective.

- **Advantages of using the first person:** It is intimate. Readers feel close to the narrator. They empathize and feel what the narrator is feeling.

- **Disadvantages of using the first person:** The narrator can only tell what she knows and cannot fill in gaps about what others are thinking or what happened when she wasn't there. We need to be wary of not shifting into other people's points of view. We can make observations about other people's emotional states based on what they say or do, but we cannot get inside their heads.

Second person: E.g., "You wake up one morning and realize you are in the wrong marriage."

- **When to use the second person:** We may want to intermittently move from the first person into the second person, as I do throughout this book. I also employed this in certain chapters in *Love in the Time of Contempt* to protect my children and avoid talking about them directly.

- *Advantages of using the second person:* This is a device that brings our reader in and asks her to stand in our shoes. It's a good trick to remember when we want our reader to lean in to the experience and feel it more directly, or we want to engage our reader in understanding that "this is a universal experience, and you know what I mean."

- *Disadvantages of using the second person:* It's tough to keep it up for an entire book—it can feel forced and tedious. We can only use it now and then.

Third person: E.g., "She was born into a family of neurotics and hypochondriacs."

- *When to use the third person:* When our memoir moves between many characters and time frames in which different things happen to different important characters. It's a version of the omniscient narrator who knows what is happening with every character and the history that precedes each character.

- *Advantages of using the third person:* We can shift between different characters' points of view. We're able to show what every character is thinking and feeling. It is less intimate and more objective. There is no need for flashbacks through a character's memory because this narrator can simply relate what happened. It is flexible—we can shift easily from one time or character to another.

- *Disadvantages of using the third person:* It is less intimate and so has a distancing effect. Our readers might find it difficult to connect emotionally with our character or characters. But if our story is more event- or plot-driven than emotion-driven, this won't matter.

The unreliable narrator: A narrative device where we want the reader to question the credibility of the narrator and wonder how much of what he or she says is true. In memoir, we can use this cleverly.

If we were writing, say, about our mental illness, addiction, delusions, or compulsive lying, we might alert our reader to the fact that we cannot be trusted to tell the truth. We want the reader to question our integrity. This narrative device helps us create within the text layers of truth, shadow, complexity, and doubt.

73

Transformation

A story is always about transformation. A character arc from point A to point B with obstacles overcome in the middle. If nothing changes between the first page and the last, there's no story. A beginning, middle, and end. Or a hook, buildup, and climax. Samuel Beckett got away with it. But he was making a point, wasn't he? About the futility of it all. We are not Beckett.

Think of your life in terms of a story arc. Were you once arrogant and self-centered but became openhearted and selfless because of some terrible accident or loss? Did you shift from grief to acceptance because you took a change of direction? Were you brokenhearted, divorced, and angry and found your way to being happily single and full of self-love?

In a story (which we all now understand memoir is), something happens—the inciting event—that bumps our story into motion. It is often something pretty horrible, something that backs us into a corner: a diagnosis of cancer, the death of a friend, the discovery of an affair, the loss of a career.

This kick-starts the transformation arc. We have to *do* something, like make a decision, act on a piece of information, end a relationship, and this reveals who we are to the reader—a complex, flawed, but lovable human being. Think active. Don't let yourself be inert.

One of the big mistakes we often make (in memoir in particular) is allowing our main characters to be passive. I made this mistake in my first novel, *The Dreamcloth*, where my protagonist, Mia, did nothing; lots of awful things happened to her. The problem is that characters who do nothing make us feel nothing. And we need our readers to feel for us.

When we write memoir, we sometimes forget that we are active players in our story. In real life, we may feel like we were victims of circumstance. But we're now in the world of story, where protagonists do stuff. So find a place in your life where you did something—stupid, brave, unforgivable. Even forgetting to call your mother back is doing something, as opposed to just ruminating.

And make sure something changes from your first page to your last. Don't make your readers wait for Godot.

74

Turning points

A life untroubled is a dull life. Our tests and trials are important moments on our time line. What makes our story fascinating is that we did not have a smooth and easy ride, that we faced conflict and obstacles. We didn't get what we wanted. So:

- What trouble have you been in?
- What have been the great trials of your life?
- When did life not run smoothly?

Identify these turning points so you can map out your life as it twisted and turned. We are who we are because of what did not go right for us. That's where we grew and became strong. In those moments we found out who we really were. We discovered what we'd tolerate and what we wouldn't. We made our moves. We took action. We survived.

We may need some of the curiosity and objectivity I spoke about earlier to identify our turning points. Even though we may have experienced our parents' messy divorce, had an abortion when we were 17, and helped raise a younger brother with Down syndrome, we may not see these as trials or tests because "that's just what happened." We may also have survived unscriptable heartaches, traumas, and abuse that we have not yet been able to name as such.

When thinking of your own life as a story, aim to identify at least three "beats" where things turned. They don't need to have been big, major moments like a death or a loss. They may be insignificant factually, but massive emotionally. Like the first time you sang on stage and got a standing ovation. Or a teacher told you she saw something in you. Or you prayed for something and got it, and so from that moment on, you believed in God.

A turning point must involve some action. Don't allow your memoir to become an internal contemplation—readers may be somewhat interested in how our emotional world developed, but they don't want to get caught up in our heads. Your story must be a balance between action and reflection (what happened and what meaning you derived from what happened). So even if you decided you were going to leave your marriage (a thought), the turning point might be "He broke the dinner plate in rage." Then show yourself calling the lawyer and filing for divorce.

Identify some of the most important turning points in your life, then reflect on why they were so important. You'll find that they were moments of transformation or crisis. These are the golden nuggets of your story. As writer Steven James reminds us, "You do not have a story until something goes wrong."

75

Them

Now let's deal with Them. The other characters in your story. Who are they? Make a list.

Each one needs to get the same fastidious treatment you'd give to characters in fiction and that you've given to yourself as the teller of the tale. Each one needs to be complex, flawed, fascinating, carefully observed, and habit-ridden and have motivations, fears, desires, and longings. We build story through character and we build character through detail.

But what if you don't know why your mother stayed with your abusive father all those years? Or why your father never told you he had a twin brother who died at birth? That's where your writer's sensibility kicks in. You can always write it this way: "It seemed as if . . ." or "I wonder whether . . ." or "I can only imagine that . . ."

We often cannot know why people in our lives behaved the way they did—perhaps they didn't know either—but we must observe them richly and compassionately, the way we would any character, and then investigate their contradictions. Do character interviews for each of them. Look at them from all different perspectives. Don't flatten them, give them depth.

Do not lapse into cliché or turn the people in your memoir into stereotypes. Allow them to be multifaceted and to reveal themselves as the story unfolds.

Figure out if you need to do some research about the people you're writing about. Don't let the research consume you, though—write first, figure out what gaps exist in your knowledge, and then go research the gaps.

Bring them to life through what they say and do

Characters give themselves away by the things they do and say, not by what they think. Thoughts (yours or your characters) are not action and do not move your story forward. Focus on action and dialogue. This is also good practice for *showing, not telling.*

Dialogue is a super-effective storytelling tool. It crafts characters, sets the pace, and shapes your story, so we should engage it with these goals in mind. It's not a good idea to use characters who lecture the reader as a way of exposition (summarizing chunks of backstory to help fill in the gaps).

Dialogue is powerful because it reveals relationships between people—the underlying tensions, currents, dynamics, and emotions. If one of your characters is a racist, bigot, or psychopath, the best way to show this is through what she or he says:

"Say that again, you moronic faggot."

"Oh darling, don't make such a fuss about things. It's terribly unattractive."

"I hate it when you walk into a room, and, like, how people stare, you know, and you feel, like, all naked and shit."

Our characters give themselves away when they speak. John, my neighbor, once said, "I go to that dentist. He's a Jew, but he's all right." Do I need to explain who he is? Nah, he did that all by himself.

We can reveal so much about our characters through speech—their social status, insecurities, and fears. Our reader should be able to "hear" their voices and feel like they're eavesdropping on a real conversation. Instead of telling the reader, "I had a difficult relationship with my mother," create a scene between the two of you and show us through the words said, interruptions, pauses, rhythms, and silences of real language what the relationship was like.

Some things to keep in mind about writing effective dialogue:

- Dialogue should move the story or plot forward. It should never be a space-filler.

- When a character asks a question, it shows what the character is feeling or thinking and allows for revelations.

- Don't state the obvious. It's not necessary for the characters to comment on events, e.g., "There was a loud bang. 'What was that loud bang?' he asked."

- The best way to learn to write dialogue is to listen to the way people speak.

- Eavesdrop. Feel the way a conversation works. It is a kind of poetry.

What we know and how we'll show

While every character needs to be richly conceived, we don't need to show the reader everything. What we show is the tip of the iceberg. What we know lies beneath the surface and remains concealed. Once we know everything we need to know about our characters, we need to make decisions about how and what we'll show our readers.

A good trick is to make two columns like this:

What I know	How I'll show it
He was broke and unemployed.	He wrote a check for $1.25 to buy a can of soda.
She was lonely and found it hard to connect with people.	She spent all her time in the garden tending to her flowers.
He was an eternal optimist.	When his blind date didn't show up, he sent her roses, saying, "I'm sure I got the time and date wrong."
He had diabetes.	He examined the ingredients on all products.

Have fun exploring your characters in this way.

76

Theme

Your life has themes. Every life does. Your work as a writer is to find those themes.

Themes are patterns that keep coming up time and time again. We can only find themes when we look at our lives objectively, when we step outside of the drama and the everyday and reflect on our life as a continuous experience. You might discover that your father leaving your mum when you were four and your marriage breaking down share a theme of abandonment or betrayal. Looking closely, you might see that there are similar themes in your friendships and work.

Perhaps you were the golden child in your family. You won awards. You were an overachiever. You always got the guy. You had it easy. You always ended up looking after others.

To find your themes, examine the important moments in your life and ask, *What was playing out here?*

This explains why my book *When Hungry, Eat* was able to touch so many people when it was ostensibly about a middle-aged woman trying to lose weight and come to terms with having left her homeland. My drama with tight clothes and flab wasn't what the story was "about." Those were the details. What it was really about was hunger. Not just physical hunger, but all hunger—the hunger of the spirit.

And everyone knows what emptiness feels like and what it's like to long for fullness. Readers who loved my book may have been coming to terms with a divorce, or with the empty nest, or with other huge life changes that made them feel exiled from the lives they once knew. Do you see how it works? The details of your story are "how" you are illustrating the themes that underlie it.

The theme is the "why" of your story. It's the foundation on which you build the rooms. The theme is the roots of your story tree. It's the place from which your story grows.

A story is not about ideas. It's about how we turn ideas into feelings. We want our readers to feel the impact of our story not in their heads but in their hearts. Theme is the magic key to unlocking that big, thumping muscle in its cage of ribs.

No matter what your story is about—what happened to you and how—it's also about something broader than the particular, deeper than the detail. All stories explore the themes that we as humans long to understand—love, death, loss, grief, injustice, beauty, horror, tragedy, innocence, suffering. Sometimes when we start writing, we don't yet have a grip on our themes, but as we write, we discover that the concrete details of say, our battle with AIDS, or coming to terms with our mother's terminal illness, are about courage, faith, loss, and grief. These are our themes and they are what make our particular story universal.

What if you don't know what your themes are when you start? That's perfectly okay—our themes may only show up once we've written a fair bit. Our themes are revealed by the obsessions or passions of our characters (which are really a form of our own obsessions or passions).

Once you've identified your themes, you can start to have fun looking for ways to reinforce them. You might notice a sub-character or an object that comes to represent the theme. In this way, you can enrich the text by exploring your theme in different ways. You can show your themes through symbolism, questions posed, setting, dialogue between characters, or characters who embody different aspects of the theme.

Theme is what helps us create the emotional connection we want with our reader: we want to evoke terror, humor, fear, intrigue, horror, delight, lust, fascination . . . something . . . anything. Theme helps us make the bridge between the personal and the universal. It's how we tap into the larger universal unconscious. The particular is only of interest to a reader if it touches emotions he or she is able to feel.

This is particularly important in memoir. For memoir to be of interest to others, it must be in service to some bigger idea or theme. Find the theme or themes that run through your story—*love overcomes fear*, or *redemption through suffering*, or *faith leads to freedom*, or *courage in the face of injustice*. Everything that happens to you in life is linked to a theme.

There are literally hundreds of themes to choose from. Here is a selection:

Alienation	Everlasting love	Isolation (physical, spiritual, emotional)
Ambition	Evils of racism	
Beauty	Faith	Jealousy
Betrayal	Family	Justice
Chaos and order	Fate	Loss of innocence
Circle of life	Good versus evil	Love
Coming of age	Greed	Love and sacrifice
Courage	Grief	Motherhood
Cruelty	Growing up	Prejudice (racism, sexism, homophobia, anti-Semitism, etc.)
Deception	Hope	
Disillusionment	Hubris	Religion
Displacement	Identity	Redemption
Escape	Injustice	Reunion

Sex	Surrender	Truth
Spirituality	Survival	War
Suffering	Trust	Youth and beauty

Spoiled for choice, right?

77

Taper

Writing memoir is about choosing the right moments, and about making powerful storytelling decisions that move the narrative forward.

The difference between autobiography and memoir is the difference between a wide-angle lens and a close-up.

Autobiography is *the story of our lives* from birth to the present day. It has length and breadth. Memoir is *a story from our lives*—it's selective, thematic, focused, and has depth. In memoir, most of the life (the canvas on which the story takes place) is implicit and disregarded.

So choose some windows from your life that reveal the part of your journey you want to explore and illuminate. Be selective. Make artistic (not narcissistic) decisions. If your story is about raising a disabled child, the fact that your father died when you were seven (which is obviously relevant to your life) may or may not be relevant to the story you're telling.

As you pick the important life-shaping moments from your life, you will begin to see themes and patterns, an almost invisible lattice of connective tissue between them. Now hold on to that thread and weave your straw into gold.

78

Telling

Our theme is our "what" (what our story is about). Here comes the how.

How will we tell our story? How will we shape the narrative? What will we include? Hide? Reveal? What order will we impose on the events? This is where our housekeeping skills come in handy. Our ability to organize and play architecturally. How we curate the experience for the reader. As Carol Shields writes in *Small Ceremonies*, "It's the arrangement of events which makes the stories. It's throwing away, compressing, underlining. Hindsight can give structure to anything, but you have to be able to see it."

Our time line (or plot) is the order of events as they happened. But the structure is how we tell what happened (what emphasis, time, and pacing we give to each thing that happened). When we write, we make choices about what to reveal and conceal, and it is this dance of disclosure and secrecy that creates the emotional journey for the reader. How we link sequences gives meaning to those moments, because all good writing builds depth as different scenes reflect off one another.

Structural decisions are big ones, and they have to be made with confidence. For example, you have to choose:

- where to start the story (what event gets the story going);

- how much emphasis to give certain parts of the story/plot;

- what point of view to use;

- what to leave out (the backstory, which is everything that preceded the inciting event that you want to use to illuminate your character's inner life);

- how to use flashbacks and memories;

- how to manage the pace (which is the way the story moves through emotional time for the reader);

- how long your story should be; and

- where to end the story.

The beginning of our story is nothing more than our careful decision about where to start the telling.

Likewise, the end is the emotional place we want our readers to end up. ("And they all lived happily ever after"—that's a beginning if ever I heard one . . .) There are many ways to lead an audience to our designated destination.

Each choice changes both the meaning of our story and the effect it has on the reader. We get to choose the particular configuration of events—like words on a page, like notes in a musical score, depending on how we want Mary to feel while she's reading our story. Our structural decisions will be influenced by our purpose in telling the story.

We move between scenes (which slow the pace down and bring readers right into the moment) and summary (narration or exposition). We pick important moments in our story for scenes, but sometimes we have to fill in gaps for readers by letting them know about something that happened outside the plot but is important to the story. We then have to quickly summarize a whole backstory or history. This is called "exposition." Exposition is a condensed way of sharing information with the reader.

There are many options for how to tell a story:

- linear—moving forward in time;

- starting with the ending and working backward (like most murder mysteries);

- the twist, where we invert the expectations we've been building all along;

- picaresque—a sequence of events or episodes moving through fascinating places or experiences;

- the story within a story, or "frame"—we frame the story, but we're actually telling someone else's story; or

- nonlinear—moving between past and present.

Each choice impacts the reader's experience. How do you decide which story structure to use?

You decide based on how you want your readers to feel at different moments.

Structure is more than what goes where.

It's the ordering of the emotional experience for the reader.

79

Tension

Think seduction.

What keeps us hooked is tension—not knowing the outcome. Will he kiss me? Will she kill him? Will she keep the baby? Who is the real father?

Every story must keep readers wondering what will happen next. The suspense arises because the reader cares about us, knows we're in trouble but is uncertain if we're going to be okay. The definition of suspense could be the anticipation of people we care about getting hurt. Writers are often given this advice: "Make 'em laugh, make 'em cry. But most of all, make 'em wait."

Our stories must create tension for the reader, the kind Hitchcock spoke about when he said, "There is no terror in a bang, only in the anticipation of it." We intensify this by structuring revelation, whether it's through drip-feeding elements of a powerful backstory that will in time explain the pain of the present, shocking our readers with the revelation of a clue, secret, or evidence, or composing a dilemma in which we are forced to face our worst fears.

Some other ways to create tension:

- foreshadow events still to come;

- have a ticking clock or a deadline (time is running out);

- hint at warnings or omens;

- insert premonitions, the "little did she know" device;

- set up story questions;

- withhold information from the reader;

- build anticipation; and

- create surprises or hint at secrets.

You need to become accomplished at teasing the reader. The opposite is boring her.

80

Touch and be touched

Albert Camus exhorted us to "live to the point of tears." What is life about, what are stories for, unless they bring us into our hearts?

We write to touch and be touched. The deepest, most sacred element of writing is that we are connecting—with ourselves and with readers. To do this, we need to be plugged into our own emotional worlds. We cannot write if we're numb to our own pain, grief, joy, lust, and longing—we have to be in touch with it all. Robert Frost wrote, "No tears in the writer, no tears in the reader. No surprise for the writer, no surprise for the reader." We have to feel it first if we want our reader to feel it second.

Our job as writers is to make readers feel something.

"But," I hear you mutter, "I can't even make my three-year-old pick up her toys, let alone get the teenager to unload the dishwasher, how do I make anyone do anything?" Of course we can't force anyone to feel anything. The only person we can make feel anything is ourselves. And the problem is that many of us are living not only a short distance away from our bodies, but a whole continent away from our hearts. For all kinds of protective, survival, and lazy reasons, many of us don't go "down there" where the feelings are. It's messy, and mucky and unpredictable. And it's sore.

No one has said it better or more concisely than Ernest Hemingway, who said, "Write clear and hard about what hurts," because "what hurts" is the connective tissue between us and our readers. They may not have buried a parent, or lost all their money, or had a father who went to jail (though that's what we're writing about), but they know loss, grief, failure, and shame. We're all visited by the same family of feelings, which arrive in the form of different life experiences. Beneath the things that transpired is an undercurrent that is not cerebral, but emotional. It joins us to all readers.

Leonard Cohen said this in an interview about songwriting:

> I think you work out something. I wouldn't call them ideas. I think ideas are what you want to get rid of. I don't really like songs with ideas. They tend to become slogans. They tend to be on the right side of things: ecology or vegetarianism or antiwar. All these are wonderful ideas but I like to work on a song until those slogans, as wonderful as they are and as wholesome as the ideas they promote are, dissolve into deeper convictions of the heart. I never set out to write a didactic song. It's just my experience. All I've got to put in a song is my own experience.

So write to touch.
While touching yourself.
Not in *that* way. You know what I mean.

81

Tell the truth

When we write, there's the danger that we might try to come across as someone we're not. To bullshit a little.

A big part of our work as writers is to see through our own bullshit. Readers sense when we're being pretentious and inauthentic and trying too hard. Writing must come from your true self. If you don't believe deeply in what you're writing, neither will your reader. As the wonderful writing teacher Brenda Ueland wrote,

> What you write today you thought and created in some idle time on another day. It is on another day that your ideas and visions are slowly built up, so that when you take your pencil there is something to say that is not just superficial and automatic, like children yelling at a birthday party, but it is true and has been tested inwardly and is based on something. . . . It must come from your true self and not your theoretical self, from what you really think, love, and believe, not from your hope to make an impression.

In addition, your true self is where your writing voice is hiding. And if there is one clear writerly goal we can successfully achieve, it's to find that voice.

But there's no concept in writing more elusive than this one. Here are some gateways in.

Why are you writing?

Why must *you* tell *this* story? Write a few paragraphs on why you and why this story. Understanding your own deep motivations will help you wrap your hands around the themes that illuminate your story. The themes are the big issues that move you. Your writing voice will always somehow be entangled in these themes.

Why you are writing is more important than what you are writing about. The what flows from the why, not the other way around. The answer to why gives you credibility (which is fundamental to your writing voice).

Make "I contact"

One of the first rules of public speaking is to make eye contact with the audience. That's how we connect and earn their trust. In writing, our challenge is to make "I contact," to tell the truth about our experience. We create trust and credibility by speaking about real things in a real way.

To do this, we have to become deep observers of our internal states and to examine our lives, the way Plato exhorted us to. It's not a quick overnight job, because we're cultivating intimacy with our deepest selves. When our writing is limp and lifeless, it's because we haven't done enough work to make "I contact."

Our writing cannot hide our experience—it reveals who we are. We have to go in deep to get to this place and stay down in the dark for a long time. We have to be in the silence until something yields. The harder we have worked to get to our own emotional truth, the more that shows up in what we write. Which is why it's easy to spot cliché and platitudes. They're recycled thoughts, regurgitated ideas. They are limp and loose because they are borrowed. They are not bespoke. They're one-size-fits-all. Our words should never have that quality. When we write, it is our chance to offer something that is truly our own.

When we do, we produce something that is the work of hard internal labor. Readers feel the sighs, the cries, the howls through which our words were born. They feel the sturdiness of deep internal roots, the clarity of a thought long mulled. They sense our writing is the product of one who has worked hard to cobble it from the cliff face of experience. As they read it, there's a kind of recognition, as something deep in their psyches arches toward it with a "yes." It has the ring of truth to it. It's not trying or posturing.

The writer Julia Cameron says, "Finding our voice has to do with finding our safety." Safety comes from trust. We learn to trust that what we say has value when we are not trying to belong to an experience dishonestly.

Anyone can learn the craft of writing, but it takes courage and guts to go deep within and explore our own chaos. We can only shepherd our readers as far and as deep as we have been willing to go ourselves. How far are we willing to go? Only we can answer that question.

But in asking it, we enter a new conversational territory with ourselves. We listen closely and discover levels of consciousness and knowing that we have not yet tapped. We see how we have lived at high speed, never pausing to allow that hard thought or crushing feeling to reach us. We've been sublimating. Shut off. We commit to doing it differently. To going in with a lantern, a shovel, and a big, brave heart.

"I contact" is a lifelong intimacy, but these are four doorways I have found to be reliable: our senses, our emotions, our memories, and the way in which we reflect on our lives. As we move through each one, we sift through the moments we've collected that have stayed with us, the interactions we've carried, the sensual imprints, the stories—and we examine them with ferocious and forensic precision. Every memory is a threshold. Whatever makes us tremble is our teacher.

Say it your way, not in cliché

A cliché is never our voice because, by definition, a cliché is something someone else has thought or experienced. When something comes too easily or we are too glib, we're likely in cliché territory.

The antidote to cliché is to look for the ambivalence or paradox in the experience. We can ask, *What am I not seeing? What is not obvious? What is hidden or buried here?* Our original voice will involve some pairing of contradictions and the way in which we hold them. A clue about the truth of our experience is that it is never one thing. So in getting to our voice, we are often engaged in a difficult conversation with something we don't quite understand. When we work this way, we come with a spirit of inquiry and a beginner's mind.

The poet Mary Oliver reminds us in her poem "The Wren from Carolina" that all things are imbued with holiness, though some may appear in more "rascally" guise than others. Everything has depth and complexity. All things have a shadow side.

We should avoid cliché except when we want to use it deliberately to play into a convention. Our writing must always be self-conscious (i.e., know what it is doing).

Sentimentality is inauthentic

Sentimentality is dishonest. Motherhood isn't "wonderful" (not all the time), nor is marriage, nor is any relationship or experience. Life is paradoxical. If we write about things in one dimension, we're not telling the truth. We all know that experience is complex. If we write that an experience is only perfect or only terrible, the reader knows we haven't explored it deeply, we've only skimmed along the surface. Some writing can get away with this—short, entertaining articles in newspapers or Sunday magazines, for instance. Some travel writing. Some romance fiction. If we are writing in one dimension, we must be doing so knowingly.

Some guidelines for telling the truth:

- the first thing we write is a gateway to go deeper;

- if it's not grounded in our own felt experience or emotion, it's not our truth;

- if it feels scary to say out loud, we're on the right track;

- if it's a cliché, it's a cop-out;

- if it's sentimental, we're romanticizing (and suppressing something);

- if it feels risky and our heart is racing, we're making progress;

- if it doesn't make sense, we're getting closer;

- ideas alone are not our voice—the head and the heart have to travel and meet at a mutually agreed-upon place;

- if we don't know how it will turn out and we feel lost, we invoke the spirit of Wendell Berry's words in which he reminds us that it is precisely when we have lost our way that we have come to our real work, and that our true journey has begun.

- if it's only one thing (great, awesome, tragic, desperate), it's unexamined; and

- if we start off already knowing the answer, we don't have a way of inquiring into the truth of the experience.

82

Timbre

The timbre of something is its resonance. Perhaps what the poet Gerard Manley Hopkins might have called "inscape."

INSCAPE: The uniqueness, individuality, self-hood of all living things. The order, pattern, unique beauty at the heart of things. The very essence of things.

According to Hopkins, everything has its own inscape—its essence, its marked individuality, and this is the elusive quality of the writing voice that we're chasing. It's often hidden in the same way that our internal organs remain mysteriously concealed. We often don't know what we're looking for.

The timbre of our writing voice is our writing style, flair, brand, fashion. It's how readers recognize and come to know us. It's our writing personality, an indescribable blend of our life experience, history, idiosyncrasies, neuroses, sensibilities, and self-awareness. It sparkles with our humor, insights, and felt experience. As the poet Mark Nepo writes, "If I had experienced different things, I would have different things to say." So getting to the timbre of our writing voice is when we find the thing inside us that wants to be said in the way that only we can say it. Our writing voice is a beautiful medley of craft (which we learn) and some ineffable part of us (our soul, if you like). It may be invisible, hidden, silent, but it's there. It's the part that Dr. Seuss describes in *Happy Birthday to You!* as "you-er than you."

Our writing voice emerges from that you-ness.

Finding our voice is the combination of our willingness and capacity to:

- feel the things that have happened to us as deeply as we can;

- use the craft of writing to evoke the emotional experience in such a way that others can feel what we felt; and

- find a bridge from the utterly personal to the universal so our experience will have meaning and significance for a reader.

We capture this timbre when we harvest whatever is buzzing deep inside us. It is our particular way of making sense of the world. Our writing voice may be hiding behind cliché, grief, convention, or clutter. Grab a shovel and clear the way. Finding your writing voice can be messy. There will be fallout, and some darlings will have to die in the process.[1]

To find the timbre of our voice, we must stay in our bodies (be present); feel deeply; remember (however we remember), and then, in the words of William Stafford, weave "a parachute out of everything broken" and create the connections that tie the chaos and despair together. We don't find it until we start writing. It's a glorious gift bundled into the experience of apprenticing ourselves to this inner work.

Our authentic writing voice is fresh, vivid, passionate, and personal. How do we know when we've found it? We know. It's like falling in love. It is clear and bright—as if our spirit stepped out of our skin and onto the page. Our writing voice is never forced. It is a perfect balance between effort and grace. Some of it is earned, some of it is given.

---

1. In his lecture "On Style," delivered in 1914, Arthur Quiller-Couch said, "Whenever you feel an impulse to perpetrate a piece of exceptionally fine writing, obey it—whole-heartedly—and delete it before sending your manuscript to press. *Murder your darlings.*"

We can work backward. Our writing voice is also what we want people to say about our writing, e.g., "passionate," "edgy," "dark," "satirical," "humorous," "quirky," "fresh." Once we know, we can become those things, inhabit those adjectives.

83

Transition

O ur readers don't really care if we lost weight or got over our homesickness. They want to know how they can learn to live with hunger and get over their own grief. They're looking for points of connection, echoes of their own experience in our stories. We succeed when we connect with them, when we bridge the personal and speak with a universal voice. That's when we make the transition.

Here are three ways I know to do this:

- always ask whether a particular event or moment is serving your story and your reader;

- make space in your text for a reader. This is an editing job. Allow breathing space in the text so that the reader's own experience can enter through the latticework of your words. Your writing must be porous, not dense like concrete; otherwise it becomes suffocating and, in the words of the wonderful Israeli writer Nava Semel, there's no way for a reader's "soul map" to enter the text;

- work toward exquisitely personal universal statements. You achieve these when you take your unique experience (nursing a dying parent, watching your marriage fall apart, losing all your money) and distill a truth that speaks to all human experience. Readers will then experience it as if you've touched on their particular experience.

Goethe said, "The Poet should seize the particular, and he should, if there be anything sound, thus represent the universal."

When we write, we're not looking for what is the same in our experience as everyone else's, but what is unique. As readers, when we stumble across an exquisitely personal universal statement, we get a gush of oxygen. Poetry is full of them. Poets are in the business of devising these sorts of offerings. It's like sipping nectar.

This connection is almost energetic, auric. It's as if the truth in me responds to the truth in you.

In an interview, Cheryl Strayed, author of the memoir *Wild*, said:

> When we see a painting that we love, we're not standing there think-ing about the artist who made it—we're thinking about how that painting makes us feel, what that reflects to us about our lives and the world. And so I love when art exceeds . . . its creator, which is the whole goal of art . . . , when it becomes not about the person who created it, but about the people who consume it.
>
> This is *especially* true in memoir, when you're writing about your-self—it has this horrible, false reputation of being the narcissistic form, which I think is pure bullshit. No good memoir is really *about* the writer—and yet it's deeply about the writer.

She reminds us that, as writers, our job is to learn how to "use [our] life as material for art" so that our lives become the raw material from which we craft something that is not for or about us, but for and about our readers.

Here are a few from my memoir, *When Hungry, Eat*:

> When we are far from those we love, we can use that as a metaphor for how far away we are from the self we can learn to love better.

and

Be patient with hunger. It is precious. We can love things more for the smallness of our portion.

and

I understood that "going back" was an illusion that prevented me from going forward. Inside my own body, I was already home.

84

Trust revisited

The pull to the page is what gets us writing. But it takes time before things click.

Often we read what we've written and we sink inside. The words aren't right. There's a breach between the longing inside us and what we're able to produce on the page. Maybe we really are no good at this. Do we have zero talent? Who did we think we were anyway, trying to write a book?

Keep diving, going down, and if you come up empty-handed, go back down for another look.

Our writing voice clicks when our ability with language finally meets that longing. It's like when two opposite sides of a magnet finally connect.

It's just like when we start learning a new language. At first our efforts will be clunky, we'll trip over the grammar, use words incorrectly and in not quite the right context. But with time and practice, as our ears and tongues become accustomed to the language, we begin to flow, we don't overthink every time we speak, we slide into the language and feel as if it's speaking through us. Connecting with our writing voice is like this.

Have you ever tried to learn a musical instrument? I did—at the age of 45 I decided to learn to play the guitar. At first I had to think each time I played a chord. I couldn't imagine putting all the chords together and actually playing a song. I kept making mistakes. It felt less like making music and more like weight lifting. But with time and practice, I eventually got into a rhythm. It began to feel graceful and breezy.

Writing gets like that too. With time and practice. It is part exertion, part grace. We control the effort, but we must yield for the grace bit.

You'll know it when it happens. The words will come out right. They'll match the longing. They'll speak rightly and make sense of the rumblings in your heart, the marvelous chaos of sense, emotion, and memory that have pulled you to the page.

Our voice is both natural but it is also crafted. It is like the perfect pitch.

85

Traveled

My father once told me I have no sense of humor. I do take life a bit on the serious side.

Yet my writing has been called "hilarious" and "laugh-out-loud funny." What this means is that I'm much funnier on the page than I am in real life.

So who am I on the page? It's not my raw, spontaneous personality, but rather a version of my personality funneled, refined, through the distillery of my craft. That filter is also carefully structured to be a conduit to a particular reader. Our voice must always be powered by the consciousness of the question, that almighty important question: *How will this connect with my Mary?*

Our personality on the page is carefully constructed. It's the version of ourselves if everything we thought and felt was first allowed to ferment and work its way through our consciousness into words. Writing is not a spontaneous expression, but one that travels a long way—through our experience, through the body, through the heart, through the head, and eventually through our hands onto the page.

It's our personality, well traveled. It's been on a journey through consciousness and craft.

Don't trust the untraveled voice.

There's a beautiful poem by Kenneth Koch called "One Train May Hide Another" that is based on a sign he saw on a railway track in Kenya. This poem forms the foundation of much of my teaching. In it, Koch reminds us that each thing in our lives—each moment, event, person—may "hide another." We need to stop and wait to allow them to pass to see what has been patiently hiding behind them all along.

Finding that authentic voice might just be about waiting to see what was already there. Often our real writing voice is hiding behind what we first write.

Though our true voice is made of everything we know about ourselves, it also has a mysterious element to it. It may not fully be the "you" you present to the world, but the you tucked away inside you. Many of us haven't even met this part of ourselves.

We have to travel to meet it, to retrieve lost selves left behind or repressed, or our imagined other selves living out a fantasy. The encounter can feel bewildering, like meeting a contradiction, but in the words of Walt Whitman:

> Do I contradict myself?
> Very well then I contradict myself,
> (I am large, I contain multitudes.)

The self that is complete has integrated ambivalence and paradox and is comfortable with things not quite making sense because they are not one thing or another but both, or many, or at odds: ordinary and miraculous. It's the "AND," not the "OR" maneuver. Romantic and dreary. Holding both grief and lightness. It's this exertion of holding two things that don't belong together that creates a heart space of inquiry. We drop out of one dimension. We see through many dimensions. We don't flatten, we expand:

I am a loyal married woman and I am a free gypsy spirit belonging to no one but myself.

When we speak from this place, we speak in truth. As a traveler who has been there and returned with new eyes.

86

Teachers

What if you don't know where to start looking for your writing voice?

That's where teachers come in. Books are your teachers. Other writers are your teachers. As much as we find our voice through an intimacy with our own writing practice, we must also read—all the time, and different things. Sometimes by reading the way others write, we feel an echo in ourselves, or see a lighthouse guiding us closer to our own voice. Find writers whose prose lights up your blood like a match to sambuca. The kindle to finding your voice is somewhere in there. Find writing that stirs and awakens you.

Write down the names of 10 writers you love and why. What you love is a clue, it's calling something forth from within you. Read lots of memoir. See how others have done it. Copy them at first to get a feel for how they write.

And know that's just the beginning.

In all spiritual stories, the search for the treasure that takes heroes on journeys far, far away is seldom about the outward journey. The treasure is back home, within. The outward journey is simply the catalyst for the inner one. But we can only get to the inner journey when we have completed the pilgrimage of exile. If we haven't exhausted the tourism of our search, we'll forever be thinking, *Maybe it's just on top of that next mountain*, or *Maybe I should read one more book about how to write.*

To find our writing voice, we must travel outward in order to find our way back into our own hearts.

87

Ten thousand hours

As human beings, we have the right to be loved, warts and all, just for who we are. But not when it comes to our writing. People do not have to love our writing just because it comes from us. We get no special love from a reader. We have to earn it. As writers, it's not enough that we just write. There is an act of creation and craftsmanship that is not just about blurting out the first thing that pops into your head and squirting it onto the page.

Good writing has worked its way through the skin, the body, the heart, the brain, the mind, and out through the hands. It's a journey of 10,000 hours of scraping away the static, clutter, rust, and cliché from our voice. Only then does it embody the gnarly grit of experience sanded down 'til it's sheer and silky as glass. It has the suppleness and confidence of the yoga teacher's flow, not the shaking jerkiness of the novice saluting the sun. It is the jazz musician who understands the medium and whose music seems effortless, but whose hours of dedication are felt imperceptibly in every note.

As Toni Morrison writes, "I rewrite a lot, over and over again, so that it looks like I never did. I try to make it look like I never touched it, and that takes a lot of time and a lot of sweat."

To get to a place of smoothness, where all the effort and time are concealed, we must dedicate ourselves to writing.

During our 10,000-hour apprenticeship, we sometimes access a moment of grace, and we catch our voice like a wave or a bird on a breeze. We enter flow, where there is a conscious, practiced ease. Our voice knows itself, and when we're with our voice, it knows. It's that kind of knowing we're searching for in our writing.

88

Texture and tone

To make our story real and rich, we want to create texture. We do this by making sure we and our other characters are not clichés or stereotypes; that we dance between light and shadow; that we do not look for neat answers to the questions our life throws up. We want to engage all the senses—to evoke the times, the moments, the situations our story is about.

Here are some techniques we can draw on:

Exposition and scenes

Sometimes we need to move the pace of the story along quickly, so we summarize events for the reader. This is called exposition or narration. But when we need to slow things down and zoom in, we intersperse the exposition with scenes, using dialogue and action to show the people and the places in our story too.

Showing and telling

You don't write about the horrors of war. No.
You write about a kid's burnt socks lying in the road.
— *Richard Price*

Don't tell me the moon is shining;

show me the glint of light on broken glass.

— *Anton Chekhov*

The reading experience should offer your readers the chance to understand your story through their own eyes. As writers, we want to leave spaces for the reader to fill in: not too big and not too small. Enough space for imagination, but not so much as to become obscure.

When we show, we paint an image for the reader (like in movies) so the reader gets to interpret and feel her own emotional response. This is how we create rich, vivid text that is open to interpretation. It makes writing inviting, not didactic.

The movie director David Mamet talks about telling the story

in cuts . . . through a juxtaposition of images that are basically uninflected. . . . A shot of a teacup. A shot of a spoon. A shot of a fork. A shot of a door. Let the cut tell the story. Because otherwise you have not got dramatic action, you have narration. If you slip into narration, you are saying, "you'll never guess why what I just told you is important to the story." It's unimportant that the audience should guess why it's important to the story. It's important simply to tell the story. Let the audience be surprised.

When writing about emotions and senses, we should aim to show rather than tell. Telling robs the reader of his or her own emotional take on the situation. It flattens instead of expanding the text.

Hemingway said, "If a writer . . . knows enough about what he is writing about he may omit things that he knows and the reader, if the writer is writing truly enough, will have a feeling of those things as strongly as though the writer had stated them. The dignity of movement of an iceberg is due to only one-eighth of it being above water."

The difference between telling and showing:

Telling	Showing
He was angry.	He clenched his jaw, curled his fists, and rose to his feet.
She was grief-stricken.	Something cold flickered inside her; memories of her mother moved like minnows beneath a dark surface.
He felt relieved.	He couldn't stop the sigh that escaped his lips.
She is lonely.	She looks for a familiar face, but never sees one.
He felt hot.	Large half-moons of sweat grew at his armpits.
Justin was nervous.	Justin couldn't lock eyes with Catherine. He fumbled with his grey polyester tie, which only seemed to choke him up more.

Showing takes the reader right into the moment, into the memory, the emotion. Telling the reader what we remembered, felt, and saw summarizes, but does not allow the reader to emotionally connect with our story.

Metaphors

Well-chosen metaphors can enrich our writing. Too many metaphors make it seem like we're trying too hard. Our writing should never get in the way of the reader and draw too much attention to itself. It should serve the story; otherwise it's just showing off.

Metaphors extend our meaning by making interesting and unusual connections between things that are not usually connected, such as "the skateboard of my heart," "the regatta of her moods," "spelunking in my obsession," "the jagged glass of his caress."

Of his stroke, poet Tomas Tranströmer writes, "I am carried in my shadow like a violin in its black case."

In *Beloved*, for which she won the 1993 Nobel Prize for Literature, Toni Morrison describes a crucial moment between Paul D and

Sethe, in which he confronts her with the atrocity of what she's done (which I'm not going to tell you, because that would be an epic spoiler and you really do need to read this book), Morrison writes: "Right then, a forest sprang up between them, trackless and quiet."

Terry Pratchett, the late English author, instead of describing a dog as "revolting and smelly," describes it as "halitosis with a wet nose."

Beautiful writing viscerally ignites our senses and stokes our imagination.

Once you begin to investigate language, you will want to play with all its riches and craft something beautifully textured that is utterly your own.

89

Tenderness

In one of the great anthems of the modern era, "Can I Get an Amen," celebrity drag queen RuPaul sings that if we don't love ourselves, we're not going to be able to love anyone else.

But what exactly does "loving ourselves" mean?

It means giving ourselves a break. Dropping the judgments. Accepting our swirling imperfections. And letting a bit of kindness seep in.

All writing begins with just this kind of self-compassion.

To write, we have to own our voice and our right to write. I sometimes think that writing is an act of dynamic empathy—for ourselves and for others. In life, we're often caught up in opinions, reproaches, and criticisms. Our culture teaches us to analyze, disparage, and bring others down to size. We ridicule people who make mistakes and vilify people on social media who disagree with us. Satire and some journalism are built on the impulse to demolish. This energy, as much as it is powerful and necessary in propaganda and in persuasive writing, is belittling and, at its core, arrogant. It is built on the idea of "them" and "us." The subtext is, "You are so stupid, and look how clever I am." Its impulse is to destroy.

This judgmental outlook is especially unhelpful for memoir writers. When we write our stories, we're looking at ourselves and our lives as if we were watching ourselves in the mirror. But those are the same eyes that silently judge: *I'm so fat. Are those new wrinkles? I wish I was prettier, I wish my teeth were straighter, my nose were smaller, my eyes less slanty . . .*

While these voices inside our head may be difficult to tame, and may be the soundtrack to our lives, what is certain is that no one (not even our mothers) is interested in reading this kind of self-directed hate speech.

Van Jones, who was a close friend of mine when we were at Yale together and is now a CNN commentator, once said it to me like this—"No one trusts self-hating politics"—when I expressed to him my shame at being a white South African Jewish woman who came from privilege. What he meant was "Get over it—do the work you have to do to come to some place of peace with who you are—and then you are ready to do political work."

Writing requires us to do the same, whether we're writing about ourselves or about other characters. To write complex characters (where the character is not a cliché), we have to see all their facets— the heroic and the cowardly; the loyal and the lustful. Remember: we don't have to write about our pain, but we have to write from it. In memoir, we may choose not to expose our self-loathing, shame, guilt, anger, resentment, and fear, but we have to know them intimately to write authentically about ourselves. And if ever we choose to go on to write fiction, we need intimate knowledge of the emotions we're attributing to the imaginary characters we conjure up.

If we want to write—about ourselves or other characters—in a way that connects us to our readers, we have to be connected to ourselves. This means dropping the judgment and replacing it with compassion.

Think about it: if we write about ourselves with condemnation and criticism, or, alternatively, we skim over difficulties with platitudes, we almost render ourselves unreliable narrators—readers will feel our discomfort with who we are and find it hard to connect with us emotionally. Whereas, if we look at our wounded places with a soft gaze, and write about what we find difficult about being ourselves with tenderness, readers cannot help but connect with us. The upside too is that we give others permission to look at their own wounds with that same gentle regard.

90

Takeaway

Please do not write your story to teach anybody anything. Your job in writing your story is not to lecture people or give advice.

Does this mean your story won't impart anything or have a message? Of course not. There should always be a "takeaway" for the reader.

But we don't want to assault our readers with our "message." We are more sophisticated and subtle than that. We want to tuck it into the storytelling, secret it into our themes, stitch it into the structure. We want to show what we've learned and how we learned it. But we must allow our readers to draw their own conclusions and decide what meaning they can take from our experience to enrich their lives.

Since we are always asking, *What's in it for the reader?* and we're always thinking about Mary, we must make the transition from the personal to the universal. Simply by wrestling with our material and making meaning from our experiences, we will have a takeaway message for our readers. We don't want it up in flashing lights, but slipped between our lines, like a subliminal message, that softly creeps into our reader's heart when she puts our book down and sighs.

How do we know what the takeaway is?

We figure it out as we write our story. Our lives are filled with teachable moments; we just haven't acknowledged them as such yet.

Writing our story is partly about recognizing the journey we have been on, harvesting the wisdom from our own lives and making it relevant to others. Every life is a commentary on existence—and ours is as insightful, rich, and meaningful as anyone else's, including Buddha, Jesus, Moses, Stephen Hawking, Bill Gates, and Michelle Obama.

Here are examples from other books:

The pathos and the gift of life is that we cannot know which will be our defining heartbreak, or our most victorious joy.
— Alexandra Fuller, *Cocktail Hour Under the Tree of Forgetfulness*

You live inside your parents' lives until, one day, they live inside yours.
— Donia Bijan, *Maman's Homesick Pie*

Maybe what we say to each other is not so important after all, but just that we are alive together, and present for each other as best as we can be.
— Anne Lamott, *Some Assembly Required: A Journal of My Son's First Year*

Once we realize that our ordinary experience has this potential to offer huge insight into all of existence, we start to pay more attention to our lives. We become more curious, respectful, mindful. We learn our place in the great family of things.

Mary Oliver's poem "The Swan" describes in exquisite detail a swan flying through the sky, and ends with three astonishing lines that point us to feel how a single beautiful image "pertains to everything," and how this recognition is enough to bring us toward both an understanding of what beauty is for and an impulse to change our lives.

Don't try too hard for a takeaway. As you write, ask yourself these questions:

- What have been the biggest "aha" moments of my life?

- What am I proud of?

- What can I do better than anyone else?

- What have been my wake-up calls?

- What have I survived (big and small)?

- What do I know now that I wish I'd known back then?

- If I had to write my autobiography in six words, what would they be?

Your story is as much about what you believe—about life and all the craziness that happens in it—as it is about what has happened to you. Think of the events as merely the catalysts or prompts for you to share with the reader what you make of this strange, wonderful, heartbreaking, illuminating existence.

91

Top and tail

Write your beginning and your ending. You can do this right at the end because by now you will understand the emotional journey you want your reader to take with you. Where do you want to find them and where do you want to leave them?

You want your opening lines to:

- draw the reader right into the action, to place them in the middle of the story;

- hook the reader into wanting to know more;

- make the reader care about you;

- give the reader confidence that she is in the hands of a reliable storyteller;

- introduce your reader to a fascinating world or character; and

- shock, grip, or in some other way be emotionally compelling.

I opened *When Hungry, Eat* with this line: "I wish I'd never kept this appointment."

Here are some great opening lines from memoirs:

I was sitting in a taxi, wondering if I had overdressed for the evening, when I looked out the window and saw Mom rooting through a Dumpster.
— Jeanette Walls, *The Glass Castle*

I have a son my son is dead I had a son.
— Kate Shand, *Boy*

If you had met my father you would never, not for an instant, have thought he was an assassin.
— Magda Szubanski, *Reckoning*

It took me a long time and most of the world to learn what I know about love and fate and the choices we make, but the heart of it came to me in an instant, while I was chained to a wall and being tortured.
— Gregory David Roberts, *Shantaram*

My father and mother should have stayed in New York where they met and married and where I was born. Instead, they returned to Ireland when I was four, my brother, Malachy, three, the twins, Oliver and Eugene, barely one, and my sister, Margaret, dead and gone.
— Frank McCourt, *Angela's Ashes*

And your ending?

Leave your reader with your message or some story that holds your message. *When Hungry, Eat* ends like this:

People we love may be diagnosed with horrible illnesses, die in car accidents or become paralysed. . . . These things may indeed happen to us. Life is uncertain. All we can know is that the uncertainty remains, flickering like an infinite ember in the kiln of this incarnation.

Faith steers us towards finding a shelter amidst the uncertainties of life. . . . Faith is the labour of returning to this search. This nurturing of the space hallowed by our attention is a daily affair. A moment-by-moment devotion.

We do it one breath, one mouthful at a time.

What final words do you want to leave your reader with? What last taste do you want to leave in the mouths of their souls?

PART V

Then What?

Congratulations! You've just completed your manuscript. It's champagne cork–popping time.

This sets you apart from 99 percent of other people who want to write a book. Finishing shows you're committed, you have stamina, and you can set a goal and reach it.

Now go for a walk. A swim. A naked walk in the moonlight (what the heck, you've just FINISHED your draft—you're a god!).

We'll talk about what's next when you come back.

P.S. Don't forget to celebrate.

92

Tragic drafts

Okay, I know you thought you were done. And you are. With the first draft.

But—please stay with me on this—writing a book is like climbing a mountain. As soon as we reach the peak we've been aiming for, we look ahead and see there's another peak ahead. And, frankly, we're buggered and don't know if we've got it in us to get there.

That's why we need to take that break. Step away. Do some knitting. Go on holiday. Make a scrapbook. Read *Fifty Shades of Grey*. Because what we've actually finished is our "shitty first draft," a phrase coined by Anne Lamott in her fabulous book *Bird by Bird* (which is on the list of "Urgent Books to Help You Learn the Craft" in the appendix at the back). I prefer to call it the "tragic draft." First drafts always are. It's in their nature. The problem lies in our expectation that first drafts should be good.

Think of the first time you tried anything—a kiss (how sloppy, how where-the-hell-should-the-tongue-go?); a recipe (overcooked, raw, unflavored, soggy in the middle); a musical instrument (how the hell can it be so hard to strum?). Why do we expect that our first writing attempts will immediately sing on the page? They will be clumsy. Our drafts will be verbose. They will tell too much and not show at all and we won't even know the difference. There will be sinkholes of cliché, minefields of passive voice, and we'll think everything we've written is so marvelously profound and prize-winningly perfect. Our first drafts will suck in all these ways. They are meant to.

The problem is when we think it means *we* suck. Our tragic draft joins forces with our inner critic and soon we're feeling like we'll never write again. And that we ourselves are absurdly tragic.

I prefer to call our tragic first writing attempts "wabi-sabi drafts." *Wabi-sabi* is a Japanese term, derived from art, which denotes the beauty of that which is imperfect, impermanent, and incomplete. We can learn so much from our broken attempts, from our ineptness and misshapen inelegance. We can grow in acceptance and compassion and find the joy in effort and grace. The questions I ask writers about their first drafts are:

- What is imperfect about this draft?

- What is incomplete about it?

- Where are the cracks?

- Where is the wisdom and beauty in this draft?

And, more important: what do you love about this draft?

Find what you love in what is broken and the brokenness will become part of the story you are telling.

93

Tidy, tighten, trim, and tuck

What begins to rescue our first tragic draft is this part: the tidying, tightening, trimming, and tucking.

This is where we go back to the words. Each and every one. This stage is sometimes called "the rewrite," but in truth, we often rewrite as we're working on our first drafts. Once we have a version of our first drafts—printed out and ceremoniously filed or bound—we must now return to the manuscript with the aim of strengthening our sentences and polishing our writing. As the author George Saunders writes, "The struggle to improve our sentences is the struggle to improve ourselves. . . . Working with language is a means by which we can identify the bullshit within ourselves (and others). If we learn what a truthful sentence looks like, a little flag goes up at a false one." It matters how we come to this process. If we come grumbling and miserable to the task, we lose the chance to love the words and sing the prose into shape. In truth, I have come to appreciate this part of the writing process more and more with every book I've written, and it has (quietly) become my favorite (*she whispered*).

Every time I reengage with a piece of writing, I remember that my love of language was inspired by the poet Dylan Thomas. From him I learned that the words we choose create a landscape of experience for the reader.

Later in life, in reading writers like Hemingway and J. M. Coetzee, I felt the power that comes from an economy of language. By choosing my words carefully, I assembled my identity not haphazardly but with architectural vigilance. As I found the right word, one after the other, the experiences the language was carving sharpened. Light refracted through the faceted crystal of each sentence. I understood my life better.

When we compress our language, we are forced to make bold choices: what will suffice? What is enough? Beautiful compression is the art of holding back, saying less, scaling down. We must write with as much detail as we can about the moments, people, events, places, and experiences that have shaped our lives. But each detail must serve the story. Writing is a process of refining what we are saying. It is a series of endless decisions.

Here are some ways to improve our writing:

- By shortening and varying our sentences. Shorter sentences are often preferable to long, rambling ones. Intersperse long ones with short ones by culling the qualifiers (e.g., "somewhat," "quite a bit"), which weaken writing; we don't want too many.

- By losing obvious words like "happy," "sad," "good," "bad." Find the worthiest word, the one that packs the most power. Mary Oliver reminds us to "look for verbs of muscle, adjectives of exactitude."

- By continuing to ask, *What am I saying?* Writing is the process of winnowing your thoughts and emotions down to get rid of wobbles, lumps, and fuzziness. We know we've understood what we're writing about when we can nail it down to one sentence.

- By making the reader care. Structure a series of hooks or unanswered questions that keep your reader emotionally engaged. As soon as the reader stops caring, you don't have a reader.

- By avoiding anything fancy. Aim to write like you talk.

- By staying in the active voice, unless the passive is serving a useful purpose of making the agency of the subject invisible or sublimated. Every sentence should have a subject, verb, and object, in that order. If you use the passive voice, e.g., "The door was opened," rather than "He opened the door," make sure this is a conscious writing decision.

- By going light on adjectives and adverbs, which are often accessories cluttering our sentences when their meaning can be absorbed by a more potent verb or noun. If an adjective or adverb is casting a surprising or ironic light, then keep it, such as in "killing me softly" as opposed to "killing me brutally," or "a cold beauty" rather than "a stunning beauty."

- By working out when to show and when to tell.

- By keeping tenses stable: hold on to the reins of your tenses so they don't stray mindlessly between the past and present and confuse your reader.

- By always writing for and toward a reader (remember Mary?). Don't be obscure or pretentious. Stand in the reader's shoes. Read through her eyes. Is what you've written fascinating, useful, or entertaining?

- By zooming in and out. Good writing is textured—it moves from the specific to the universal and from the abstract to the specific. If you're writing about the impact of bad eating habits on general health, you can describe a McDonald's burger and the person eating it. If you're writing about taking out the trash, make it about a deeper truth—that every so often, we have to get rid of our emotional junk.

- By staying in one skin. Pick a point of view and stick to it. If you're writing in the first person, you can't know what other people are thinking or feeling, but you can imagine or suspect, e.g., "It was as if she was looking for faith, scrambling and failing."

- By remembering that when you've finished writing, you're not finished. Rewriting is a crucial (and fun, enlivening) part of the writing process where you bring left-brain thinking and ask logical, analytical questions like: *Does this make sense? Have I left something out? Does one line follow logically from the next? Can I say this better? Is there a more perfect word to describe this?* Reshape, resculpt, eliminate. Writing generally improves with every word we cut.

- By applying the "mattress principle"—sleep on it. Step away from the writing and let it settle. Writing needs time. The time a grain of sand needs to turn into a pearl.

- By asking yourself when you're done, *What am I really saying here?* Sometimes we change in the writing, and what we end up saying is several degrees off what we began wanting to say. You then need to pull the narrative threads tightly through the text to make your work appear seamless.

- By reading it aloud. Sometimes you can hear what works and what doesn't more easily when you hear the words read out loud rather than just reading the text on a page.

If you're wondering how long your story should be, apply the Goldilocks principle. Most books are between 60,000 and 90,000 words.

But it's never the quantity of words that counts. It's the quality. When it comes to each book, there's a Baby Bear in there somewhere—where it's not too short and it's not too long (though I would always err on the side of less).

94

The third eye

Our tragic first drafts are now ready for The Third Eye.
The first eye is, of course, our first draft. The second eye is our
own editing and rewriting. But there comes a time when we need a
third eye. Like of another human being.

It's hard enough to be brave and heartfelt and spill our guts on
the page. Now comes a new round of resilience. We've had courage in
private, when our writing was for our eyes only. Now we have to go
public. And this is where many great writers falter. The fear of what
others will say or think is crippling. They shy away from the edge.

There will come a time in the life of your book when you think,
That's it, I'm done. And what this is, is the heart saying, "I have given
everything I have to this work." While you may be "done," your work
is not. This is exactly the point in time when you need fresh eyes on
your words. Eyes of someone who does not love you as a brother, sister, spouse, lover, or friend. But someone who will look at your words
dispassionately and let you know whether your words "work" or need
more work.

Successful writers seek feedback on their writing. Until and
unless you have given your work to a person who is qualified to comment on the quality of your work, your writing exists in a vacuum.
You cannot know if it works for a reader, or just for you.

Pick that person carefully. Just like you wouldn't ask your sister to diagnose whether those spots on your legs are chicken pox, you shouldn't ask her what she thinks of your manuscript. In the same way as your hairdresser is not qualified to fill a cavity in a tooth, he is equally unqualified to pass judgment on your writing.

I always choose carefully those to whom I show my work. Family members, husbands, and best friends are out. Why ask your spouse or girlfriend (who has never read a memoir) to appraise your work? We will learn nothing constructive from indiscriminate praise. When we show our writing to someone, we need suggestions about how to improve our writing, not blanket assertions about how gifted and talented we are.

Find a professional. If you value your work, you must pay a professional person who charges for their time to give you their feedback. Find someone whose work you respect. A connection with the right person is essential. You have to trust their feedback. Find out what they've written. Find out if they're published authors themselves.

Brace yourself to hear that your writing still needs more work. Feedback builds resilience. And to survive as a writer, you need to be a warrior.

This next phase is called "the rewrite."

Hidden peaks

I hope it's helpful to know up front that the first draft hides the rewrite. Please don't be put off, as overwhelming as it may feel. Trust me when I say that you will find the resolve and energy to re-tackle the manuscript. It's almost as if only by finishing our first draft and standing there looking ahead do we manage to pull together the muscle, spirit, and heart to forge ahead.

A manuscript assessment will give you a structural edit. This is a big picture analysis of whether:

- our characters are believable, sympathetic, interesting enough, and the character arc works;
- our plot has flaws, holes, or logic issues;
- our writing voice works;
- the pace, setting, and point of view all feel right; and
- the structure (how we've chosen to tell our story) is effective or could be changed.

The assessment is not necessarily an edit or a proofread, because your book is not ready for that yet. It will only be ready when you have done your rewrite.

So what is the rewrite?

The rewrite is where you take your raw draft and you make it stronger. You create more sinew in the text, you weave more deftly, you deepen your voice, you shorten your waffling. You find one better word for the four you have chosen to describe the weather.

How to rewrite

There are a couple of ways to learn to rewrite:

- keep working at your own writing and rework it;
- do a short course on editing;
- get professional feedback (it's hard to learn to rewrite on your own);
- step away from your work so you come back fresh (or trick yourself into making it look new by changing the font or printing it out and reading it on paper instead of on the screen); or
- read your work aloud and listen to how it sounds.

95

Toughen up

When we've been brave enough to seek out the third eye and we've given our writing to someone to review, we may expect a reward for our courage. Like positive feedback. Sometimes their feedback will feel like a dagger to the sternum. That's because we were hoping to hear that this is the best thing that's ever been written.

Invariably we will be told that there is still a lot of work that needs to be done. Feedback will include valuable suggestions about how to improve the manuscript. It will feel like a personal affront. It isn't. It's just feedback. We can choose to use it or not. When deciding whether to use it or not, we need to park our ego outside.

Here are some ways I've learned to respond constructively to feedback on my writing:

- Brace yourself: I've made the mistake of expecting praise, and I have learned that it takes much less time to recover from the shock of an editor's report if you have no expectations. No matter how many years you have worked on a book (my first took me 10 years), expect to do a rewrite. Assessors do not modify their responses to manuscripts based on how long it has taken us to produce it. They probably don't have a clue about how long we've worked on our book. The manuscript is assessed on its merits. So the fact that we feel we've "done the hard yards" is irrelevant. There will be more work. And this is not because assessors, editors, and publishers are mean. They want our book to be the best it can. With fresh eyes on our manuscript, we'll get invaluable perspective that we, having lived inside the forest of our manuscript and unable to see the wood for the trees, simply don't have.

- Be realistic: Every single manuscript benefits from a good edit. We know that as human beings we are works in progress—all of us profit from a little work on ourselves, whether physically, emotionally, or spiritually. Treat your manuscript as a work in progress. I received a 23-page report from my publisher on the first draft of my book *Things without a Name*. Twenty-three single-spaced pages. By the end of my rewrite, those 23 pages had become my map toward a book I could never have written without that feedback.

- Keep your poise: Never take critique or feedback personally. Any feedback that is not pure praise makes us want to scuttle back into the shell of our craft and hide there forever. Because writing is an act of courageous self-disclosure, our egos are intricately tied up in our work. But this is where we have to exercise the greatest self-restraint and maturity. The feedback is on our story, not on us.

- Some editorial feedback can be undiplomatic and harsh. Some editors need to show how clever they are. Others are gentler and understand that it is more helpful to offer useful suggestions than to bludgeon someone's manuscript. Expect the worst. If necessary, do as I do and get your husband or someone near to you to read the report first and to prepare you with "This is gonna hurt," or "This isn't so bad, really."

- Give yourself time: Step back and give yourself at least a week to absorb the feedback. If a report has really hurt you and damaged your self-esteem as a writer, you need to let the sting pass so you can look beyond the hurt to the substance of the report. As with all things that make us feel small, we need to give ourselves a little time to bounce back.

- Evaluate dispassionately: This is only one person's opinion, and all opinions are subjective. Who wrote the manuscript? You did. Well done! What did the assessor or editor do? They read it. Anyone can read a manuscript. Not everyone can finish one. If you hate everything in the assessment, accept that your opinion is equally valid. However, there is the small factor of your hurt pride, which could be clouding your judgment. The auditions for the television series *American Idol* show us that sometimes we don't know we can't. Let someone more objective than you read the report and ask them, "Is there anything valuable here?"

- Use methodology: Work through the critique with a highlighter looking for gems. Do not dwell on the words that have hurt you. Look for constructive suggestions about story line, characterization, use of language, and keep notes as you go through the report. Make a list of suggestions in the report that you do not agree with. If, for example, you feel the editor has not understood the point of the book, use this constructively to ask how you might better have crafted the manuscript so that your intention was clearer. We are in control of the story, and so if someone fails to respond to it, we need to go back and look at how to rework it so we can successfully communicate our story.

- Become unattached to your previous ideas about the book: Sometimes we need to let go of what we thought would work best in the story. If the editor has suggested that your story needs to start in a new place, while you may not agree, why not try to start the story here this time round and see how you go? It is not useful or helpful to be adamant about things that are not crucial. Ask yourself if it would totally distort the story if you started it in a different place. Would it matter very much if you cut out that section the editor thought was gratuitous? Some things can be shifted without us losing our sense of what we are trying to achieve in the manuscript.

- Fight for the heart of your story: While the aim should be to work openly and constructively with feedback, you do not have to roll over and accede to all the suggestions in the report. This is still your book. And your vision for it is what drives it. While a story can have a limb moved here and there, a bit of plastic surgery, fight for its heart. Fight to retain what you think is crucial to your story. There may be parts of the report you just don't agree with or that reflect the editor's own agenda and not yours.

- Recommit and begin again: When you're ready, take a deep breath and start on the rewrite. How badly do you want this book published? How hungry are you? How hard are you prepared to fight for it? Does your book deserve your attention and devotion? Then get over the editorial report and use it as a stepping-stone to a more wonderful manuscript.

- Finally, keep these things in mind:

  - It's just writing—it either works or it doesn't work.

  - Don't take feedback personally.

  - Don't be precious about what you've written.

  - Be grateful for feedback; it gives you the chance to look again. Writing is all about looking again, going deeper.

96

The last word

Tell a story so you can give it to another person.
A story is a public act of communication.

— Maxine Hong Kingston

One of the most important books I ever read as a law student was
Patricia Williams's *The Alchemy of Race and Rights*. The book
opens with this line: "Since subject position is everything in my analysis of the law, you deserve to know that it's a bad morning."

What Professor Williams is saying right there is: there are no
right answers in law. It's all about subject position—how I see it,
where I'm coming from. It's quite an incendiary statement because
lawyers and legal professors believe that objectivity and certainty are
the cornerstones of legal thinking.

I was a terrible lawyer. A tragic legal thinker. I had too much
empathy, was distracted by "irrelevancies" such as the fact that an
accused person had been beaten by the "victim" (her abusive husband)
for years before she shot him in the back of his head (unprovoked, in
the eyes of the law).

So critical legal theory was formative for me because of the way it challenges legal norms of logic and structure that merely reflect and reinforce existing (and often invisible) power relationships in society. It taught me that in all matters of thinking, there are many paths. Writing is no different. There is no one way to write, to be inspired, to become a success. There are many ways, and probably the best way is your way.

If you're like me, you love to read about how your favorite authors work, what their writing rituals and habits are, how many hours they spend at their desks, or how many words they write in a day. When we're starting out, we may think to copy them, imagining they must have the magic formula for how it's done. This is a good place to begin, but as we mature as writers, we become more conscious of our own processes, and this is when we start to make our own path. I express this in *When Hungry, Eat*:

> What others can teach us through their experience is only useful to a certain point. When we recognize where that point is, that's when our authentic experience begins.

Understanding how we write, how we become inspired, and what works for us is part of the writer's journey. No one can tell you how your creativity works. No one can offer a formula that will show you how to work your voice. Trust yourself. Learn everything you can from others. Then walk your own path.

For your story to touch others, write fearlessly. Write through your pain. It is the prism through which your story is refracted. In the moment of your honesty lies your greatest power. Resting in your pain is the key to every other heart that has been broken.

Never doubt that your personal story can change someone else's life. Our stories, fearlessly told, are lanterns that light the path for others to be fearless.

I believe in the power of writing. We script our lives by the words we choose, the way we line them up one after the other, like glass beads on a page or screen. When we write our journey, we learn more deeply who we are, we share our insights with others, we help others make meaning, we stay close to who we are inside, we help others find bridges across experiences, we help hold the world together in an invisible web of words.

Writing is an act of sharing—we work hard to get the right words onto the page so that we can share emotions and experiences with others. We reach people in faraway places, we meet people who have long since died, and we enter our own inner worlds—worlds we could never have reached had we not written our story. Writing gives us the chance to be generous; we can make the world a better place, by sharing.

Writing and sharing our stories is the bravest, most generous act of service we can perform.

Go be brave.

You are braver than you think.

Appendix

Urgent Books to Help You
Learn the Craft

Big Magic: Creative Living Beyond Fear by Elizabeth Gilbert, Riverhead Books, 2015

Bird by Bird: Some Instructions on Writing and Life by Anne Lamott, Pantheon Books, 1994

Do the Work by Steven Pressfield, Domino Project, 2011

The Icarus Deception: How High Will You Fly? by Seth Godin, Portfolio/Penguin, 2012

If You Want to Write by Brenda Ueland, Graywolf Press, 1987

On Writing: A Memoir of the Craft by Stephen King, Scribner, 2000

On Writing Well: An Informal Guide to Writing Nonfiction by William Zinsser, Harper and Row, 1976

The Right to Write: An Invitation and Initiation into the Writing Life by Julia Cameron, Putnam, 1998

Still Writing: The Perils and Pleasures of a Creative Life by Dani Shapiro, Atlantic Monthly Press, 2013

Wild Mind: Living the Writer's Life by Natalie Goldberg, Bantam, 1990

Writing for Emotional Impact by Karl Iglesias, Wingspan Press, 2005

The Writing Life by Annie Dillard, Harper and Row, 1989

Writing Tools: 50 Essential Strategies for Every Writer by Roy Peter Clark, Little, Brown, 2006

Bibliography

Bernhard, Toni. *How to Be Sick: A Buddhist-Inspired Guide for the Chronically Ill and Their Caregivers*. Boston: Wisdom, 2010.

Berry, Wendell. *Collected Poems, 1957–1982*. San Francisco: North Point Press, 1985.

Bijan, Donia. *Maman's Homesick Pie: A Persian Heart in an American Kitchen*. Chapel Hill, NC: Algonquin Books, 2011.

Block, Peter. *The Answer to How Is Yes: Acting on What Matters*. San Francisco: Berrett-Koehler, 2002.

Bly, Robert. *A Little Book on the Human Shadow*. Memphis, TN: Raccoon Books, 1986.

Brown, Brené. *The Gifts of Imperfection*. Center City, MN: Hazelden, 2010.

Cameron, Julia. *The Right to Write: An Invitation and Initiation into the Writing Life*. New York: Putnam, 1998.

———. *The Vein of Gold: A Journey to Your Creative Heart*. New York: Putnam, 1996.

Cixous, Hélène. *Three Steps on the Ladder of Writing*. New York: Columbia University Press, 1993.

Cook, Molly Malone, and Mary Oliver. *Our World*. Boston: Beacon Press, 2007.

Deraniyagala, Sonali. *Wave*. New York: Alfred A. Knopf, 2013.

Enright, Anne. *Making Babies: Stumbling into Motherhood*. London: Jonathan Cape, 2004.

Fedler, Joanne. *The Dreamcloth*. Johannesburg, South Africa: Jacana Media, 2005.

———. *Love in the Time of Contempt: Consolations for Parents of Teenagers*. Richmond, Australia: Hardie Grant Books, 2015.

———. *Things without a Name*. Sydney, Australia: Allen & Unwin, 2008.

———. *When Hungry, Eat*. Sydney, Australia: Allen & Unwin, 2010.

Fitzgerald, F. Scott. *My Lost City: Personal Essays, 1920–1940*. New York: Cambridge University Press, 2005.

Ford, Debbie. *The Dark Side of the Light Chasers: Reclaiming Your Power, Creativity, Brilliance, and Dreams*. New York: Riverhead Books, 1998.

Forster, E. M. *Aspects of the Novel*. London: Edward Arnold, 1927.

Frank, Anne. *The Diary of a Young Girl*. London: Constellation Books, 1952.

Frankl, Viktor. *Man's Search for Meaning*. Boston: Beacon Press, 1963.

Fuller, Alexandra. *Cocktail Hour under the Tree of Forgetfulness*. New York: Penguin, 2011.

Geisel, Theodor Seuss. *Happy Birthday to You!* New York: Random House, 1959.

Goethe, Johann Wolfgang von. *Conversations of Goethe with Eckermann and Soret*. London: Smith, Elder, 1850.

Hemingway, Ernest. *Death in the Afternoon*. New York: Charles Scribner's Sons, 1932.

Huxley, Aldous. *Brave New World*. Garden City, NY: Doubleday, Doran, 1932.

James, Steven. *Story Trumps Structure: How to Write Unforgettable Fiction by Breaking the Rules*. Cincinnati, OH: Writer's Digest Books, 2014.

Joyce, James. *Dubliners*. New York: B. W. Huebsch, 1916.

Jung, Carl. *Alchemical Studies*. R. F. C. Hull, trans. Princeton, NJ: Princeton University Press, 1967.

King, Stephen. *On Writing: A Memoir of the Craft*. New York: Scribner, 2000.

Kinnell, Galway. *New Selected Poems*. Boston: Houghton Mifflin, 2000.

Koch, Kenneth. *The Collected Poems of Kenneth Koch*. New York: Alfred A. Knopf, 2007.

Lamott, Anne. *Some Assembly Required: A Journal of My Son's First Year*. New York: Riverhead Books, 2012.

Mamet, David. *On Directing Film*. New York: Viking, 1991.

McCourt, Frank. *Angela's Ashes: A Memoir*. New York: Scribner, 1996.

Mehl-Madrona, Lewis. *Narrative Medicine: The Use of History and Story in the Healing Process*. Rochester, VT: Bear, 2007.

Morrison, Toni. *Beloved: A Novel*. New York: Alfred A. Knopf, 1987.

————. *What Moves at the Margin: Selected Nonfiction*. Jackson, MS: University Press of Mississippi, 2008.

Myss, Caroline. *Why People Don't Heal and How They Can*. New York: Harmony Books, 1997.

Nepo, Mark. *The Book of Awakening: Having the Life You Want by Being Present to the Life You Have*. Berkeley, CA: Conari Press, 2000.

Oliver, Mary. *Blue Pastures*. New York: Harcourt Brace, 1995.

————. *Red Bird: Poems*. Boston: Beacon Press, 2008

————. *Swan: Poems and Prose Poems*. Boston: Beacon Press, 2010.

————. *Why I Wake Early: New Poems*. Boston: Beacon Press, 2004.

Parks, Tim. *Teach Us to Sit Still: A Skeptic's Search for Health and Healing*. New York: Rodale, 2011.

Pratchett, Terry. *Men at Arms*. London: Gollancz, 1993.

Purpura, Lia. *On Looking: Essays*. Louisville, KY: Sarabande Books, 2006.

Rapp, Emily. *The Still Point of the Turning World*. New York: Penguin, 2013.

Rich, Adrienne. *On Lies, Secrets, and Silence: Selected Prose, 1966–1978*. New York: Norton, 1979.

Rilke, Rainer Maria. *Rilke's Book of Hours: Love Poems to God*. Anita Barrows and Joanna Macy, trans. New York: Riverhead Books, 1996.

Roberts, Gregory David. *Shantaram*. New York: St. Martin's, 2004.

Saunders, George. *The Braindead Megaphone*. New York: Riverhead Books, 2007.

Shand, Kate. *Boy: The Story of My Teenage Son's Suicide*. Johannesburg, South Africa: MFBooks, 2013.

Shields, Carol. *Small Ceremonies*. New York: Penguin, 1996.

————. *Unless*. London: Fourth Estate, 2002.

Spiegelman, Art. *Maus: A Survivor's Tale*. New York: Pantheon Books, 1986.

Spock, Benjamin. *The Common Sense Book of Baby and Child Care*. New York: Duell, Sloan and Pearce, 1946.

Stafford, William. *The Way It Is: New and Selected Poems*. Saint Paul, MN: Graywolf Press, 1998.

Stobezki, Eldad. "Nava Semel on Literature, the Creative Process, the Relationship between Literature and Lyric Opera, on Editing and Deleting." *This Century's Review*, February 2006. http://history.thiscenturysreview.com/Nava_Semel_on_literature_the_creative_process_the_relationship_between_l.nava-semel.0.html.

Szubanski, Magda. *Reckoning: A Memoir*. Melbourne, Australia: Text Publishing, 2015.

Thomas, Dylan. *Under Milk Wood: A Play for Voices*. New York: New Directions, 1954.

Tolstoy, Leo. *Anna Karenina*. New York: T. Y. Crowell, 1889.

Tranströmer, Tomas. *The Great Enigma: New Collected Poems*. Robin Fulton, trans. New York: New Directions, 2006.

Ueland, Brenda. *If You Want to Write*. 2nd edition. St. Paul, MN: Graywolf Press, 1987.

Walls, Jeannette. *The Glass Castle: A Memoir*. New York: Scribner, 2005.

Warren, Frank, comp. *PostSecret: Extraordinary Confessions from Ordinary Lives*. New York: ReganBooks, 2005.

Whiteley, Opal. *The Singing Creek Where the Willows Grow: The Mystical Nature Diary of Opal Whiteley*. New York: Penguin, 1995.

Whitman, Walt. *Song of Myself*. Mineola, NY: Dover, 2001.

Whyte, David. *River Flow: New and Selected Poems 1984–2007*. Revised ed. Langley, WA: Many Rivers Press, 2007.

Williams, Patricia. *The Alchemy of Race and Rights*. Cambridge, MA: Harvard University Press, 1991.

Acknowledgments

I am grateful to the many talented people who brought their expertise to this book. Nicole Abadee assessed the manuscript with her fastidious eye before Roz Hopkins and Natalie Winter of Captain Honey helped me self-publish the first edition, which had a short but happy life.

My wonderful agent, Greg Messina of Linwood Messina Literary Agency, didn't flinch when I told him, "If you're sending this manuscript out, I'm only interested in Hay House." I am indebted to him for the secret efforts agents make without any guarantee of an outcome, but which brought us this edition. It reminds me that people who work with authors do it because they love books. And that weirdly gives me hope for all of humanity.

Thanks to the team at Hay House, including Patricia Gift for saying YES, Leon Nacson of Hay House Australia for breakfasts and banter, Anne Barthel for her brilliant editorial input which reshaped and improved this book, Marlene Robinson, the marketing team, and all those who have touched this book in ways both apparent and invisible. You have all indelibly left your heart prints here. Thank you for your care, curation, and confidence in *Your Story*.

A Few Things about Me

I've written nine books in just about every genre (literary and commercial fiction, self-help, narrative nonfiction, and memoir, but not crime fiction or erotica—yet). Some have been international and #1 Amazon bestsellers.

My books have sold over 650,000 copies worldwide and have been translated into different languages, including Czechoslovakian, where my name was changed to Fedlerova, and Korean, in which I couldn't work out where my name was on the cover.

I am a speaker, writing mentor, and writing retreat leader. Each year I take a group of women to Fiji, Bali, or Tuscany to learn the craft and develop the consciousness for writing. See www.joannefedlerwritingretreats.com for details.

Through my WINGS program (Words Inspire, Nourish and Grow the Spirit), I run a series of Author Liftoff workshops for aspiring authors as well as a free seven-day writing challenge and my eight-week online Author Awakening Adventure: www.authorawakening.com.

This book is the culmination of 10 years of writing and teaching others to write. I hope it offers you many ways into your story. To get in touch and be on my mailing list for special offers, you can e-mail my team at admin@joannefedler.com.

If you'd like to download the workbook I've created as an accompaniment to this book, please go to www.joannefedleryourstory.com.

Hay House Titles of Related Interest

YOU CAN HEAL YOUR LIFE, the movie, starring Louise Hay & Friends
(available as a 1-DVD program, an expanded 2-DVD set,
and an online streaming video)
Learn more at www.hayhouse.com/louise-movie

THE SHIFT, the movie,
starring Dr. Wayne W. Dyer
(available as a 1-DVD program, an expanded 2-DVD set,
and an online streaming video)
Learn more at www.hayhouse.com/the-shift-movie

* * *

THE COURAGE TO BE CREATIVE: How to Believe in Yourself, Your Dreams and Ideas, and Your Creative Career Path, by Doreen Virtue

SH#T YOUR EGO SAYS: Strategies to Overthrow Your Ego and Become the Hero of Your Story, by James McCrae

WHAT LIES BEYOND THE STARS: A Novel, by Michael Goorjian

WRITING FOR MY LIFE: Reclaiming the Lost Pieces of Me,
by Nancy Levin

YOU HAVE 4 MINUTES TO CHANGE YOUR LIFE: Simple 4-Minute Meditations for Inspiration, Transformation, and True Bliss,
by Rebekah Borucki

All of the above are available at your local bookstore,
or may be ordered by contacting Hay House (see next page).

* * *

We hope you enjoyed this Hay House book. If you'd like to receive our online catalog featuring additional information on Hay House books and products, or if you'd like to find out more about the Hay Foundation, please contact:

Hay House, Inc., P.O. Box 5100, Carlsbad, CA 92018-5100
(760) 431-7695 or (800) 654-5126
(760) 431-6948 (fax) or (800) 650-5115 (fax)
www.hayhouse.com® • www.hayfoundation.org

———

Published in Australia by: Hay House Australia Pty. Ltd.,
18/36 Ralph St., Alexandria NSW 2015
Phone: 612-9669-4299 • *Fax:* 612-9669-4144
www.hayhouse.com.au

Published in the United Kingdom by: Hay House UK, Ltd.,
The Sixth Floor, Watson House, 54 Baker Street, London W1U 7BU
Phone: +44 (0)20 3927 7290 • *Fax:* +44 (0)20 3927 7291
www.hayhouse.co.uk

Published in India by: Hay House Publishers India,
Muskaan Complex, Plot No. 3, B-2, Vasant Kunj, New Delhi 110 070
Phone: 91-11-4176-1620 • *Fax:* 91-11-4176-1630
www.hayhouse.co.in

———

Access New Knowledge.
Anytime. Anywhere.

Learn and evolve at your own pace
with the world's leading experts.

www.hayhouseU.com

Free e-newsletters
from Hay House, the Ultimate
Resource for Inspiration

Be the first to know about Hay House's free downloads, special offers, giveaways, contests, and more!

 Get exclusive excerpts from our latest releases and videos from *Hay House Present Moments*.

 Our *Digital Products Newsletter* is the perfect way to stay up-to-date on our latest discounted eBooks, featured mobile apps, and Live Online and On Demand events.

 Learn with real benefits! *HayHouseU.com* is your source for the most innovative online courses from the world's leading personal growth experts. Be the first to know about new online courses and to receive exclusive discounts.

 Enjoy uplifting personal stories, how-to articles, and healing advice, along with videos and empowering quotes, within *Heal Your Life*.

Sign Up Now!

Get inspired, educate yourself, get a complimentary gift, and share the wisdom!

Visit www.hayhouse.com/newsletters to sign up today!

you can

HEAL YOUR LIFE ♥

make your soul smile

Visit HealYourLife.com daily and meet the world's best-selling Hay House authors; leading intuitive, health, and success experts; inspirational writers; and like-minded friends who will share their insights, experiences, personal stories, and wisdom.

♥ **DAILY AFFIRMATIONS**   ♥ **UPLIFTING ARTICLES**
♥ **VIDEO AND AUDIO LESSONS**   ♥ **GUIDED MEDITATIONS**
♥ **FREE ORACLE CARD READINGS**

FEEL THE LOVE...

Join our community on Facebook.com/HealYourLife

www.HealYourLife.com®